Praise for
Executable Specifications with Scrum

"This is a great book that demonstrates the value of putting effort behind requirements in an Agile environment, including both the business and technical value. The book is well-written and flows nicely, approachable for both the manager and the developer. I am recommending this book to all Scrum teams who need to integrate business analysts and architects as active teammates."

—**Stephen Forte**, Chief Strategy Officer at Telerik and
Board Member at the Scrum Alliance

"Cardinal's book brings to light one of the most important and neglected aspects of Scrum: Having user stories that are ready to sprint. Teams often complain about this, and the author offers practical advice on how to get it done right!"

—**Steffan Surdek**, co-author of *A Practical Guide to Distributed Scrum*

"*Executable Specifications with Scrum* doesn't shine through its depth but its breadth. This compendium of proven agile practices describes an overarching process spike touching important aspects of product development in a cohesive way. In this compact book, Mario Cardinal clearly explains how he achieves a validated value stream by applying agile practices around executable specifications."

—**Ralph Jocham**, Founder of agile consulting company effective agile. and
Europe's first Professional Scrum Master Trainer for Scrum.org

"Cardinal provides deep insights into techniques and practices that drive effective agile teams. As a practitioner of the craft Cardinal describes, I now have a written guide to share with those who ask, 'What is this [ATDD/BDD/TDD/Executable Specification/etc] thing all about?' Regardless of the name de jour, Cardinal gives us what works."

—**David Starr**, Senior Program Manager, Microsoft Visual Studio

"Scrum is barely a process, only a framework. It is a tool, and you have to provide many complementary practices to reach true business agility. This book is perfect for teams that are using Scrum and want to learn about or get started with executable specifications."

—**Vincent Tencé and François Beauregard,** Scrum Trainers at Pyxis Technologies

"This book maps out the important place of specifications in an agile landscape to the benefit of agilists of all roles."

—**Erik LeBel,** Technology and Development Consultant at Pyxis Technologies

Executable Specifications with Scrum

Executable Specifications with Scrum

A Practical Guide to
Agile Requirements Discovery

Mario Cardinal

✦✦Addison-Wesley

Upper Saddle River, NJ • Boston • Indianapolis • San Francisco
New York • Toronto • Montreal • London • Munich • Paris • Madrid
Capetown • Sydney • Tokyo • Singapore • Mexico City

Library of Congress Control Number: 2013939927

ISBN-13: 978-0-321-78413-1

ISBN-10: 0-321-78413-8

Text printed in the United States on recycled paper at Courier in Westford, Massachusetts.

First printing, July 2013

Editor-in-Chief
Mark Taub

Executive Editor
Chris Guzikowski

Senior Development Editor
Chris Zahn

Marketing Manager
Stephane Nakib

Managing Editor
Kristy Hart

Senior Project Editor
Lori Lyons

Copy Editor
Apostrophe Editing Services

Senior Indexer
Cheryl Lenser

Proofreader
Paula Lowell

Editorial Assistant
Olivia Basegio

Cover Designer
Chuti Prasertsith

Senior Compositor
Gloria Schurick

To my four outstanding children:
Dominic, Lea-Marie, Romane, and Michael.

Contents

Contents

Figure List

Preface

There is a wide range of books that have been written about specifications. Unfortunately, most of them are not useful for software development teams. These books rely on traditional engineering practices. They assume requirements are known upfront and, once specified, will not change for the duration of the project. And if changes happen, they presume they will be minor, so they could be tracked with a change management process. They promote a sequential process starting with a distinct requirements phase that delivers a detailed requirements specification before starting to design and build the product.

Goal of This Book

It is my belief that traditional engineering practices are not suitable for software development. Central to the process of software specification is a high level of uncertainty, which is not the case with traditional engineering. Fortunately, with the growth of the agile community in the past decade, a body of knowledge more suited to the reality of software development has emerged. Many books explaining agility have become must-read books for anyone interested in software development. A large majority of them contain at least a chapter or two on requirements, some almost totally dedicated to this topic. Because I believe these texts are important, I will include citations from them and reference them throughout this book.

I wrote this book to add to this body of knowledge. It is a compendium of the agile practices related to executable specifications. Executable specifications enable us to easily test the behavior of the software against the requirements. Throughout this book, I will explain how you can specify software when prerequisites are not clearly defined and when requirements are both difficult to grasp and constantly evolving. Software development practitioners will learn how to trawl requirements incrementally, step-by-step, using a vision-centric and an emergent iterative practice. They will also learn how to specify as you go while writing small chunks of requirements.

This book aims to explain the technical mechanisms needed to obtain the benefits of executable specifications. It not only provides a sound case for iterative discovery of requirements, it also goes one step further by teaching you how to connect the specifications with the software under construction. This whole process leads to the building of executable specifications.

It is important to recognize that even with the best intentions you cannot force agreement upon stakeholders. The following African proverb explains this succinctly: "You can't make grass grow faster by pulling on it." When knowledge is incomplete and needs are constantly changing, we cannot rely on approaches based on traditional engineering. Instead, it is critical that you emphasize empirical techniques based on the iterative discovery of the requirements. The objective sought is not only to solve the problem right, but also to solve the right problem—this is the paramount challenge of software construction.

This book is unique in that it teaches you how to connect requirements and architecture using executable specifications. You learn how to specify requirements as well as how to automate the requirements verification with a Scrum framework. As a result of reading this book, you can select a tool and start using executable specifications in future agile projects. Here are five advantages to reading this book:

- You can understand how the work of business analysts changes when transitioning from traditional to agile practices.

- You learn how to groom emergent requirements within the Scrum framework.

- You get insight about storyboarding and paper prototyping to improve conversations with stakeholders.

- You discover how to build an emergent design while ensuring implementation correctness at all times

- You can understand that software architects who are adopting agile practices are designing incrementally and concurrently with software development.

Who Should Read This Book?

Readers of this book have already adopted the Scrum framework or are transitioning to agile practices. They understand the fundamentals of agility but are unfamiliar with executable specifications. They want to understand why the executable specifications are useful and most important how to start with this new practice.

With the massive adoption of Scrum framework, the next major challenge facing agile teams is to integrate business analysts and architects as active teammates. Anyone who is a Scrum master, manager or decision maker who faces this challenge should read this book. In addition, all team members involved in agile projects will benefit from this book. It goes without saying that business analysts and software architects will be happy to find a book that directly addresses their concerns.

Advanced or expert agilists will be interested in the book's concise overview of executable specifications. They could use this book to successfully guide their teammates down this path. In addition, the terminology used throughout the book can help leaders to communicate effectively with their peers.

Road Map for This Book

Executable specifications require a change in mindset. This book focuses on this issue. Executable specifications help reduce the gap between what stakeholders want the software to do (the "What"), and what the software really does (the "How"). Executable specifications address requirements in a way that makes it easy for the development team to verify the software against the specifications and this as often as requirement changes occur.

To facilitate this change in mindset, this book offers a unique approach to the process that spans nine chapters:

- **Chapter 1: Solving the Right Problem**

    This chapter explains the need to respond efficiently to the constantly changing requirements using iterative discovery and executable specifications.

- **Chapter 2: Relying on a Stable Foundation**

  This chapter explains how to identify what will hardly change: the core certainties on which the team should rely. Those certainties are not requirements. They are high-level guardrails that ensure a solution can be built. They create a stable foundation to ensure that an iterative requirements discovery is possible.

- **Chapter 3: Discovering Through Short Feedback Loops and Stakeholders' Desirements**

  This chapter shows that to tackle uncertainties, teams must discover stakeholders' desires and requirements (desirements) through short feedback loops.

- **Chapter 4: Expressing Desirements with User Stories**

  This chapter teaches you how to express desirements with user stories and how to record them using the product backlog.

- **Chapter 5: Refining User Stories by Grooming the Product Backlog**

  This chapter explains how to groom the product backlog so that you can plan sprints that can increase the likelihood of success of the feedback loops.

- **Chapter 6: Confirming User Stories with Scenarios**

  This chapter demonstrates how to confirm user stories by scripting behaviors with scenarios.

- **Chapter 7: Automating Confirmation with Tests**

  This chapter explains how to turn scenarios into automated tests so that you can easily confirm the expected behavior of the software against the evolving specifications.

- **Chapter 8: Addressing Nonfunctional Requirements**

  This chapter teaches you how to ensure quality software by specifying nonfunctional requirements.

- **Chapter 9: Conclusion**

  This last chapter summarizes the key elements of the book.

Acknowledgments

One to whom I owe the most is Nathalie Provost, who first convinced me to write this book. Throughout this journey, she has supported me and our four children so that I can fulfill that dream.

Personal thanks are due to Erik Renaud, my business partner, with whom I have shared great discussions regarding nonfunctional requirements and collaboration boards. Similarly, a personal thanks goes out to Rob Daigneau and Stefan Surdek who provided counsel and advice on the overall book-writing process.

It is well known that learning comes through real-world experience. I want to thank the Urban Turtle team, especially Francois Beauregard, Dominic Danis, Louis Pellerin, Guillaume Petitclerc and Luc Dorval, with whom I have learned so much about Scrum, backlog grooming, and executable specifications. In the same vein, I cannot forget my adventure with Tyco and the RunAtServer team, particularly Yanick Brunet and Gabriel Labrecque, with whom I had the opportunity to experience storyboarding and paper prototyping during the construction of real software.

I would like to thank my reviewers for reading the draft copies of this book and contributing numerous comments that helped improve the book. Thanks to David Starr, Leyna Zimdars, Robert Bogetti, Jochen Krebs and one anonymous reviewer.

Special thanks are due to Leita Boucicaut for assistance in reviewing and improving the manuscript. Her ability and willingness to always find the right word is outstanding. She challenged me to make the text understandable to all, even the nontechnical readers.

Lastly, I could not have published this book without the support of Addison Wesley. Thanks to Christopher Guzikowski, the executive editor; Olivia Basegio, the editorial assistant; Christopher J. Zahn, the senior development editor and Lori Lyons, the senior project editor.

About the Author

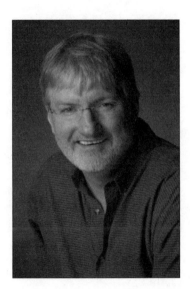

Known for many years as an agile coach specializing in software architecture, **Mario Cardinal** is the co-founder of Slingboards Lab, a young start-up that brings sticky notes to smartphones, tablets, and the web for empowering teams to better collaborate. A visionary and an entrepreneur, he likes to seize the opportunities that emerge from the unexpected. His friends like to describe him as someone who can extract the essence of a complicated situation, sort out the core ideas from the incidental distractions, and provide a summary that is easy to understand. For the ninth consecutive year, he has received the Most Valuable Professional (MVP) award from Microsoft. MVP status is awarded to credible technology experts who are among the best community members willing to share their experience to help others realize their potential.

Chapter 1

Solving the Right Problem

Agile is a group of software development frameworks that encourage rapid and flexible response to change. They are based on the practice of iterative development, where requirements and solutions evolve through customer collaboration. The Manifesto for Agile Software Development [1] introduced the term *agile* in 2001.

Scrum [2] is currently the most well-known and widely adopted agile framework. Developed by Ken Schwaber and Jeff Sutherland [3], it consists of roles, events, artifacts, and a set of rules that bind them together. Scrum enables development teams to build complex products through frequent inspection and adaptation to optimize output. The term is named for the scrum (or scrummage) formation in rugby, which is used to restart the game after an event forces play to stop, such as an infringement. In the annual "State of Agile Development" survey conducted in 2011, Scrum or Scrum variants continue to make up more than two-thirds of the frameworks being used [4]. Because of the strong adoption of Scrum, this book focuses exclusively on this framework. For those using another agile framework, the lessons of this book are generic enough to be useful.

It may seem odd to pair together the words "agile" and "specification." And it may even seem odder to write a book specifically on this topic. For many people, a specification can be paired only with "traditional" document-centric engineering practices. In an agile context, where running software is the primary measure of progress, it is easy to believe that specifications are no longer a necessity. And yet specifications are still required—more than ever. Only the nature of what is produced is different. Specifications are not only briefer but also published in a format suitable for execution on a computer—hence the name *executable specifications.*

This book aims to solve the recurring challenge encountered by many software development teams: They do not build the right software. This is a strong statement, perhaps even surprising to you. Regardless, a significant number of great software systems solved the right problem successfully. Many of them have been built by teams using the Scrum framework. I not only learned what I know about agile from these teams, but I was also a member of some of them. If you belong to one of these outstanding teams, you can recognize in this book a compendium of the practices with which you are familiar.

Unfortunately, there are still too many bloated and complex software systems. Even if all team members write code correctly, more often than not, they do not efficiently solve the actual problem. There is a distinct disconnect between what the client may want or need and what is subsequently produced. An often-quoted Standish Group [5] statistic states that 64% of the features in a typical system are rarely or never used. The exact figures from the Standish Group are depicted in the pie chart shown in Figure 1.1.

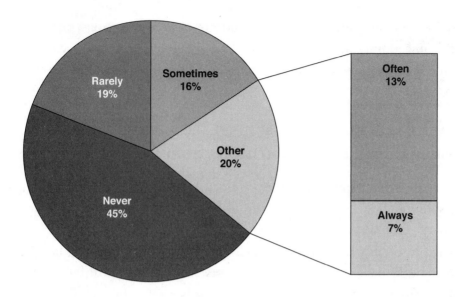

Figure 1.1 *Usage of features in a typical system.*

Looking at the pie chart, it is interesting to note that 20% of the features are always or often used. It is even more important to infer that the 80–20 rule, also known as the Pareto Principle, applies. The Pareto Principle states that, for many events, roughly 80% of the effects (output) come from 20% of the causes (input). In business, for example, it is often the case that approximately 80% of your sales come from 20% of your clients. In software development, if you correctly select the initial 20% of the requirements, this should satisfy 80% of the business needs. With ever-increasing expectations regarding usability and reliability, it is difficult to build software that does what it is supposed to do. So focus on the 20% of the features that matter. You will thus have the necessary resources to build a technical solution that meets expectations.

This chapter explains that to solve the right problem, you must first learn to distinguish the requirements from the solution. Then you must recognize the impact of uncertainty when describing requirements. This is because it is challenging to describe what needs to be built while embracing change. Finally, you can conclude that the current practices inherited from traditional engineering are inadequate in this regard. When requirements are difficult to grasp and are in constant flux, you must tackle uncertainty in a nontraditional manner. Executable specifications with a Scrum framework proved successful. This book aims to share this experience.

Distinguishing the Requirements from the Solution

Agility does not remove the need to distinguish the requirements from the solution. It is a sound practice to distinguish "What" you build from "How" you build it. Teams still need to understand the problem before solving it, even if you reduce the deliverable to a short iteration lasting less than 30 days. Only the requirements specification is different. To collaborate effectively, document only what is essential to carry out the conversation on the requirements.

Describing the "What," which is the problem that needs solving, is the core of what constitutes the specifications. Specifications define what the software needs to do, but not "How." Obviously, a specification is more than just the "What." There is the "Who," which focuses on stakeholders and the "Why" for rationalizing the way the requirements were scoped. Nevertheless, the aim remains to specify the "What," and the answers to any other questions should support this final goal.

If there are many uncertainties about the "What," the ability to easily specify the requirements can be greatly reduced, and the risk can be significantly magnified. Imagine the level of uncertainty if you need to satisfy 20 stakeholders who all have a different understanding of "What" is required. You must recognize the impact of uncertainty when distinguishing the requirements from the solution.

Recognizing the Impact of Uncertainty

The uncertainty diagram in Figure 1.2, which is a loose adaptation of Ralph Stacey's work [6], provides a graphical representation through which you can visualize the simultaneous impact of uncertainty on the "What" and the "How."

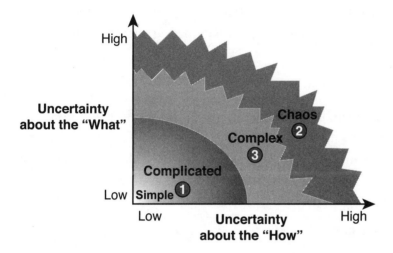

Figure 1.2 *Uncertainty diagram.*

The horizontal axis measures the degree of uncertainty about how to build the technical solution. A low degree of uncertainty is reached when a similar technical issue has been addressed or a similar decision has been made in the past. You can then extrapolate from past experience to predict the outcome of an action with a good degree of certainty. The vertical axis measures the uncertainty about requirements among stakeholders. A low level of uncertainty is reached when there is stability and predictability about which outcomes are desirable.

There are three zones of interest in the uncertainty diagram:

1. **Simple and complicated:** The traditional zone

   Much literature and theory addresses the "simple/complicated" zone. Traditional engineering practices are applicable in this zone. They involve planning specific paths of action to achieve outcomes and monitoring the actual behavior by comparing it to the plan. In this zone, the emphasis is placed on gathering data from the past to predict the future.

2. **Chaotic:** The anarchy zone

   Situations where there are high levels of uncertainty and disagreement often result in a breakdown or anarchy. This is the chaotic zone where it is almost impossible to build a solution because the traditional methods of planning, visioning, and negotiation are insufficient.

3. **Complex:** The agile zone

   This is the area on the diagram that lies between the chaotic zone and the "simple/complicated" zone. Stacey calls this large center region the zone of complexity, whereas others call it the edge of chaos. It is the zone that requires high creativity, innovation, and breaking with the past to create new modes of operating.

   With the uncertainty diagram as a backdrop, Figure 1.3 illustrates where traditional engineering practices are the most effective.

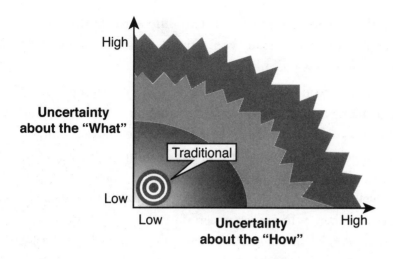

Figure 1.3 *Traditional engineering and uncertainty.*

This plan-driven approach is optimal when there is little uncertainty. In case there are many uncertainties about what needs to be built, traditional practitioners expect to achieve more predictability with an initial requirements phase and a formal change management process. They assume that uncertainty about the "What" can easily be reduced. This works fine when the level of uncertainty is not very high. Unfortunately, you can hardly apply the same recipe in the zone of complexity. When faced with complexity, your learned behavior encourages you to break the ambiguity and resolve any paradox using reductionist thinking. This may seem like the logical thing to do because it increases the feeling of being in control. However, that is far from being the case. You must use a strengthened approach.

Tackling Uncertainty

In the zone of complexity, traditional engineering practices are not effective. Making plans based on past events is not a viable approach. A more empirical approach must be taken. This is what Research and Development (R&D) practitioners have learned over the years. It does not mean that they do not plan; they just do it differently. In the zone of complexity, no matter how carefully you plan the future, it can never be more than a dream, unless you adjust your plan every day.

Here's an example to illustrate the point. Imagine if someone stated she could find the next big super-drug using a detailed and traditional plan. Would you, as an investor, be prepared to finance this multimillion dollar project based only on a plan? It is practically impossible to follow such a plan without having to continually modify it to adapt to changes. Managers as well as investors would refrain from making this volatile investment because there is too much uncertainty about the "How." Organizations have learned throughout the years that when there is a lot of uncertainty on the "How," they do not take a traditional approach.

Figure 1.4 illustrates where R&D applies in the zone of complexity. You can presume there are almost no uncertainties about "What" the requirements are. It is usually the case that there is no ambiguity about what needs to be solved. All the risks are related to the solution.

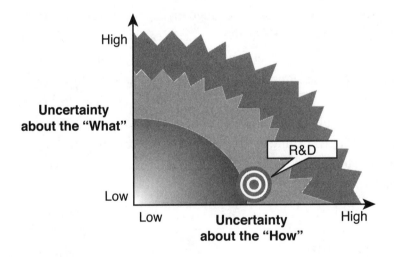

Figure 1.4 *R&D and uncertainty.*

Conversely, when almost all the risks are related to the requirements, you are in the position experienced by the majority of software development teams. Figure 1.5 illustrates this scenario. This is where using an agile framework, such as Scrum, is appropriate.

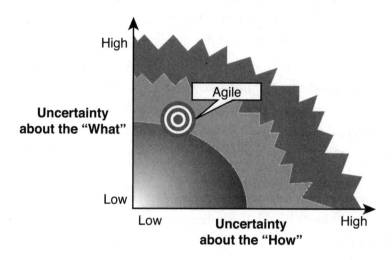

Figure 1.5 *Agile and uncertainty.*

The many thousands of signatories of "The Manifesto for Agile Software Development" have learned throughout the years that it is difficult to tackle complex uncertainty using traditional engineering practices. As a result, they promote a different strategy. The same is true for R&D. Both, R&D and agile tackle the uncertainties in a nontraditional manner influenced by the trial-and-error process. Trial and error is a heuristic method of problem solving. Only the trials that are most promising tend to be adopted and improved in future trials, whereas those that are less promising tend to be eliminated. When requirements are in constant flux, you must use iterative discovery based on a trial-and-error process.

Summary

This chapter explored why teams have difficulty solving the right problem, which is a challenge far more widespread than you might think.

It began by recognizing that agility does not remove the need to distinguish the requirements from the solution. This is still a good practice for distinguishing between the "What" and the "How."

It continued with a discussion about uncertainty and requirements. You saw that traditional specifications do not apply to software development. You determined that even with the best intentions, you cannot force agreement upon stakeholders. When requirements are difficult to grasp and are in constant flux, teams should not rely on requirements gathering inherited from traditional engineering.

Finally, the chapter concluded that teams should embrace change and adopt empirical techniques based on an iterative requirements discovery and executable specifications, which is the topic of this book.

In the next chapter, you learn that before iterating, you must clarify the things that will hardly change. This stable foundation can establish a shared vision of the solution and simplify the iterative requirements discovery.

References

[1]   http://agilemanifesto.org/

[2]   http://www.scrum.org/

[3]   Schwaber, Ken, Jeff Sutherland, (2012). *Software in 30 Days: How Agile Managers Beat the Odds, Delight Their Customers, And Leave Competitors In the Dust,* Hoboken, NJ: Wiley.

[4]   http://www.versionone.com/state_of_agile_development_
      survey/11/

[5]   http://standishgroup.com/ (2002); *Feature Usage on Typical Soft-
      ware Packages*. Boston: Standish Group.

[6]   Stacey, Ralph D. (2007). *Strategic Management and Organisational
      Dynamics*. New York: Prentice Hall.

Chapter 2

Relying on a Stable Foundation

Software is built to solve complex problems. It is naive to believe that you can write all the requirements from the start and then plan accordingly. Experience teaches you that it does not work this way. It is not realistic to think that requirements are just out there somewhere, and the only thing you need to do is get explanations from stakeholders. More often than not, stakeholders do not know exactly what they want. And if they know what they want, unfortunately they do not agree among themselves. As noted in Chapter 1, "Solving the Right Problem," when faced with ambiguous requirements, you must stop using traditional management practices and start tackling uncertainties differently.

As strange as it may seem, to master uncertainties, you should start by identifying the certainties and the thing that will hardly change. Those certainties are not requirements. They are guardrails that ensure a solution can be built. They create a stable foundation on which you can rely. They simplify the specification work and ensure you never end up in the zone of total chaos.

This chapter explains what you should do to ensure those elements of stability exist prior to the start of iteratively discovering the requirements.

Defining What Will Hardly Change

A guardrail is recognized by the team as something that rarely changes, which you can take for granted and which should be used as a guide to assist in decision making.

Guardrails not only ensure a solution can be built, but they also reduce the scope of the solution by clarifying the boundaries of what needs to be built. They provide a foundation to help the team stay healthy. Faced with constantly changing requirements that often seem unproductive, the team must stay focused to continue to perceive a meaning in the product. Guardrails recall the purpose of the product. They need to not only be shared with the whole team, but also known by each member.

Here is the list of the guardrails to put in place to provide the basis for tackling uncertainties:

- A healthy team
- The involvement of all stakeholders
- A shared vision
- A meaningful common goal
- A set of high-level features
- A "can-exist" assumption

Creating a Healthy Team

Constructing software remains an activity in which interactions between individuals are paramount. By increasing the quality of interactions between stakeholders and the team, you can reduce accidental difficulties. Unfortunately, you cannot control the stakeholders; they simply are who they are. However, you can organize the makeup of the team. You can easily influence the size, structure, and collaboration model. The easiest way to get a stable foundation is with a well-functioning team.

A team is a group of people with complementary skills linked in a common purpose. If you use the Scrum framework, you are already aware of the quality properties of a healthy team: namely, an autonomous, cross-functional, and self-organized team with fewer than 10 members who are peers.

The most important element of this team is the presence of someone devoted full time to the specification of the software. This person is accountable for the requirements specification. In the Scrum framework, this role is the product owner.

The second most important element is a development team with developers who have complementary skills and expertise. In a healthy development team, developers generate synergy through individual responsibilities and shared roles such as programmer, tester, analyst, integrator, or architect. This enables each developer to maximize his strengths and minimize his weaknesses.

The third most important element is a product owner who ensures the development team is the ultimate product. A development team does not need a solo hero who keeps his knowledge to himself. Thriving beyond the departure of various members and through multiple iterations requires shared collaboration and collective ownership. In a healthy team, the requirements specification is a common and shared asset. Even if the product owner is accountable for the specification, everyone should be involved in the conversation surrounding the requirements.

The fourth and final element of importance to creating a healthy team is a team that inspects and adapts repeatedly, using prescribed events. The Scrum framework prescribes four formal opportunities for inspection and adaptation:

- Sprint Planning Meeting
- Daily Scrum
- Sprint Review
- Sprint Retrospective

Each of these events offers the possibility for the Scrum team to inspect and adapt the work in progress. The fulfillment of these recurring events is fundamental. This is why there is a specific role, the Scrum master, for ensuring these events are understood and enacted.

Requiring the Involvement of All Stakeholders

After you have a well-functioning team, you must ensure all stakeholders will get involved in the discovery process so that the team builds the right software. From the beginning, the product owner must identify stakeholders, determine their involvement, and as much as possible, manage their influence in relation to requirements.

Stakeholders are any person, or group of people, who have an interest in your software and aren't directly involved with its construction. Basically, anyone who is not a product owner, Scrum master, or team member is a stakeholder and potentially a useful source for feedback.

In a simple world, there would be only one stakeholder, the sponsor paying for the software. This is rarely what happens in real life. Simplicity is seldom reality. Usually, there are more than a dozen stakeholders, often with conflicting needs; hence the importance of their involvement. Obviously, some will be more vocal and will try to dictate priorities. This is normal; there is always a power play between stakeholders. The product owner, however, must be attentive to everyone while respecting the political game in place.

There are two types of stakeholders involved in this iterative discovery: internal and external. Internal stakeholders are the more important of the two because they are the ones who have something to gain from the successful completion of the software. The product owner must be actively engaged with these people:

- Buyers

- End users

- Domain experts

- Sales team

- Support team

- Infrastructure and operations team

- Enterprise architecture team

- Managers

External stakeholders, such as suppliers, distributers, unions, cities, society, and the government are the ones who can positively or negatively influence the performance of the software upon completion. Even if they are a lower priority, do not ignore them.

Expressing a Shared Vision

When you have the involvement of all the stakeholders, it is essential to clarify the vision. Thankfully, because you collaborate closely with stakeholders, you are not in total chaos. You can highlight the vision early and with minimal effort. If the product owner discusses the long-term purpose and intent of the software with stakeholders, you should get a product vision on which all agree.

In a perfect world, the name of the software would summarize clearly and unambiguously the product vision. A name is people's first introduction to the software. Names are used repeatedly, and they tend to focus the mind.

Unfortunately, this is rarely the case. Names are provided by marketing departments or by the project management offices. Frequently, they are defined arbitrarily without any consideration for the product vision. They are often just a code name to easily identify the project from an administrative perspective.

Because of the administrative considerations, you can hardly ignore the official name. However, nothing prevents you from having an informal name: a one-line description that summarizes the vision. This is what is recommended.

Describe in a few words the vision of what the software needs to accomplish. This short, one-line summary should provide a shared understanding of what the software is supposed to be and do. A clear vision provides context for making better decisions and taking responsibility throughout the course of the software development life cycle. It profoundly influences the contribution of the stakeholders and the team. The team gains momentum because everyone pulls in the same direction. It is an element of stability that improves results. It affects what is produced and how people behave while producing it.

A name chosen carelessly and arbitrarily is a dangerous source of ambiguity. Similarly, the lack of a unique description about the overall vision is symptomatic of ambiguity. Do not hesitate to consolidate all the nicknames, working titles, and project definitions under one official description.

To create an unambiguous one-line summary, follow the naming heuristic popularized by Gause and Weinberg [1]. The following quote from their book concisely summarizes this three-step process:

> "First propose a name, next offer three reasons why the name
> is not adequate, and then propose another name that eliminates
> these problems."

Repeat the three-step process until a useful description is found. Remember that a perfect one-line description does not exist, so do not remain stagnant by repeating the heuristic endlessly.

Here is a demonstration of the process. Suppose the Metropolitan Transportation Authority of New York City wants to define the vision for a self-service, smartcard ticketing kiosk to be used by commuters.

The first possibility that comes to mind is a description like "Transit Ticketing Project." Here are three arguments against this choice:

1. The ticketing software doesn't specify the name of the transit authority.

2. "Project" implies that the software's utility ends with the completion of the project.

3. Nothing in the name implies anything about a self-service kiosk. (There is a self-serve kiosk.) The greatest benefit of the software is to remove the need for a salesperson to complete the transaction.

After reviewing these shortcomings, the stakeholders suggest a second choice: "NYC Metropolitan Transportation Authority Self-Serve Ticketing Kiosk," which possesses the following weaknesses:

1. You should remove "NYC" from the name because everybody knows that MTA is the transit authority of New York City.

2. The name does not imply that the tickets are uploaded to the smartcard.

3. Nothing in the name implies that the kiosk can also be used to read how many tickets are left on the smartcard.

After these two trials, the team decides to turn to a third one-line description: the "MTA Self-Serve Smartcard Ticketing Kiosk." The team could continue the critical naming process further but it decides to stop because everyone feels comfortable with this result. The objective of the naming heuristic is not only to produce a good description, but also to ensure everybody in the team has a better understanding of what the real problem is.

Expressing a shared vision is an activity directed by the product owner. It consists mainly of face-to-face meetings with stakeholders. The result is a short, one-line summary of what the software is supposed to be and do. It is a stable foundation in the sense that it should not change for at least a full year. Obviously, this is an exercise that must be repeated on an annual basis (or earlier, in the event of a major change that requires you to completely redefine the product).

Distinguishing a Meaningful Common Goal

Sometimes it is difficult for stakeholders to identify the product vision. This usually happens when stakeholders try to look too far into the future. In this case, an approach that can help is to refocus the discussion around a meaningful common goal for the coming year.

In addition to helping consolidate the vision of the product, a meaningful summary of the common goal is an important asset because it explicitly states why the software must exist from the stakeholders' perspective. What is its reason for being? Though development teams know how to build software, few know a lot about the software domain and fewer still know "Why" they do what they do. The "Why" means the driving motivation for action, the common goal that justifies the existence of the software. Making explicit the software's common goal, the "Why," helps the development team understand the stakeholders' motivations.

Identifying a meaningful common goal is usually done at the same time as the face-to-face meetings. The three-step naming heuristic—arguments against one-line summary—should be used not only to improve the goal, but also to ensure an open discussion and a shared understanding among the stakeholders. Here is the common goal for the "MTA Self-Serve Smartcard Ticketing Kiosk."

Doubling the number of points of sales without raising the operating budget

Identifying a Set of High-Level Features

A list of main features is an important binding element in creating a stable foundation. If this step is not taken, the product vision you have created so far will never be concrete. A feature is a piece of high-level functionality that delivers value to one or more stakeholders. The features list defines the boundary between the software and the outside world. It provides a shared understanding of the scope of what needs to be built. It defines the high-level requirements for inclusion in the software.

During the face-to-face meetings, the last item on the agenda should be to list the major features of the software. Because you seek to define the scope of the software, the list should be short. Make sure to enumerate only high-level items. If necessary, consolidate smaller items into something higher-level. Choose appropriate names to concisely summarize the purpose of each feature.

Here is a first cast of the list of features for the "MTA Self-Serve Smartcard Ticketing Kiosk":

1. Smartcard reading

2. Shopping cart

3. Ticket payment

4. Smartcard loading

And here is the final features list after the stakeholders apply the naming heuristic:

1. Smartcard reading

2. Ticket selection

3. Payment

4. Smartcard writing

The vision, the meaningful common goal, and the high-level features are guardrails because it is unlikely those will change rapidly. Faced with ever-changing needs, these assets are the only certainty on which you may rely in the upcoming months. They are a stable foundation upon which to discover requirements.

Now that the product owner has established a stable foundation with stakeholders, a final activity is to share this knowledge with the team.

Validating the "Can-Exist" Assumption

All software exists to solve a problem. This assumption of existence is a universal starting point that all problem solvers share. This "can-exist" assumption is present in anything humans create. Developers always start new software with the assumption that the solution exists and that the problem will be solved.

Equipped with the vision, the meaningful common goal, and the high-level features, the product owner should sit with the development team and explicitly validate with it the "can-exist" assumption. In addition to ensuring that everyone is on the same wavelength, this enables rapid detection of technical issues.

It is extremely rare that you will discover during the "can-exist" meeting that it is impossible to build the software. In this context, it may seem an unnecessary activity. Yet it must not be ignored because it is mainly intended to ensure that the vision is shared and understood by the development team.

As a follow-up of the "can-exist" meeting, the product owner should work with the Scrum master to ensure the team places the shared vision in a highly visible location so that all team members, as well as passers-by, can see it. Furthermore, when a new member joins the team, one of the first duties of the Scrum master is to communicate, in a one-on-one conversation, the vision, the meaningful common goal, and the high-level features of the software.

Summary

This chapter identified what will hardly change and how to create a stable foundation.

It began by emphasizing the importance of having a well-functioning team, as well as the involvement of all stakeholders. It continued by determining that a shared vision, a meaningful common goal, and a set of high-level features are at the heart of establishing an unambiguous and clear purpose. Because these three elements are unlikely to change rapidly, they are guardrails on which everyone can rely.

Although setting up guardrails is necessary, it is not sufficient, particularly when you are faced with situations that constantly change. Though what has already been explained may seem a bit simplistic, this is only one small step toward mastering executable specifications. Creating new software is a challenging endeavor.

In the upcoming chapters, you will learn to approach such a challenge with an open mind by using the trial-and-error principle in the form of frequent feedback loops. This can enable teams to adapt to evolving requirements and reach the end target: a successful and efficient product.

References

[1]   Gause, Donald C., Gerald M. Weinberg (1989). *Exploring Requirements: Quality Before Design*. New York, NY: Dorset House Publishing.

Chapter 3

Discovering Through Short Feedback Loops and Stakeholders' Desirements

Previous chapters determined that when there are many uncertainties about software requirements a healthy team with a shared vision, a meaningful common goal, and a set of high-level features are all necessities. This creates a stable foundation to guide the team. Expressing the product vision is only the first step in a larger process that creates successful software. For software to truly come to life, the next step is to learn how to react to stakeholders' evolving requirements. First, you apply a trial-and-error method through short feedback loops, and second, you focus on stakeholders' desires and requirements. This is the purpose of this chapter.

Applying the Trial-and-Error Method

When you are confronted with many uncertainties, you must recognize your human limitations and accept that you can hardly expect to succeed in the first attempt. Several trials will be required. The only way to succeed is to fail. Therefore, fail early and often.

Succeeding through failures is rarely promoted as a positive experience. However, if you were lucky as a child, your family encouraged you to fail early and often. If you were really lucky, your teachers did as well. Unfortunately, for the rest of us, we have been trained from grade school to always find a perfect result, as though there was an exact answer to every problem. The "Failure Is Bad!" syndrome that pervades constantly pushes us to find the perfect answer.

For the best of us, this type of conditioning leads many to develop a sense of invulnerability known as the God Complex. Wikipedia defines a God Complex as: *"a person who may refuse to admit the possibility of error or failure, even in the face of complex or intractable problems or difficult or impossible tasks."* [1] A God Complex is an absolute conviction that YOU know how the software should work. This "I-know-it-all" approach is inappropriate in a context in which there are many uncertainties about the requirements. Instead, you need to approach requirements specification with humility and use a different problem-solving technique.

In 2011, economics writer Tim Harford discussed, during a Ted Talks presentation [2], the importance of variation and selection when solving complex problems. He argued that through trial-and-error or generate-and-test procedures, which is another way to express variation and selection, you can find a solution more quickly than by using a traditional God Complex approach.

When solving complex problems, making mistakes is a perfectly natural process. As the adage goes, "to err is human." For many among us, we resist that process because it seems inefficient and erroneous. However, when looking back at history, you can find many examples in which solutions have been discovered through error, resulting in happy accidents. Scientist Alexander Fleming discovered penicillin one day through such an accident. Having left some cultures out for a period of time, he realized that fungus had grown on some of them, thereby killing the cultures. After that accidental discovery, he continued his research for another 10 years before he gave up. Not long after abandoning his project, other scientists took over his extensive research and perfected it, resulting in the antibiotics we now commonly use to cure bacterial infections. This discovery, although founded on an accident, proved to be one of the most important findings in human history.

Though Fleming's discovery was accidental, you want to aspire toward a more rigorous course of trial and error. You need to turn away from accidental discovery and aim toward deliberate discovery. Take, for example, Apple's iPod. In 2001, the iPod was created through an exhaustive process of trial and error over a period of 8 months. As explained on the website LowEndMac [3], though certain technological elements already existed to give the development team a foundation from which to work, the implementation of short feedback loops with Steve Jobs helped to bring the project to fruition.

> "Steve Jobs took a very active role in the project, scheduling frequent meetings with the directors from Fadell's group and PortalPlayer. During these meetings he would tell them in detail what issues he had with the device, whether it was the interface, sound quality, or the size of the scroll wheel."

What resulted was the most innovative portable music player on the market. Steve Jobs' team understood that to achieve the required results, it had to accept that "mistakes" would be made. It celebrated those mistakes and, as James Joyce once said, accepted that "a man's errors are his portals of discovery." This perspective is a good way of navigating through a largely unpredictable world. Keep in mind that there are no real mistakes, just learning opportunities. Each and everything you do, whether you achieve your goal, leads you to another place. When there are no instructions to follow, trial and error is an efficient path to discovery.

History shows that some of the biggest and most influential inventors followed the same path. As Thomas A. Edison once said, *I haven't failed; I have just found 10,000 ways that didn't work.*

The problem-solving procedures of trial and error previously described can be used in other, more artistic, situations as well. Take music, for instance. In music creation, the artist often pursues an exploration sequence that starts at the inception of the idea and continues until she is satisfied with the finished product. The music may come first, just as the lyrics may be the beginning of the process. Adding and subtracting musical instruments, arrangements, and vocals are part of the trial-and-error process that can lead to some of the masterpieces you enjoy to this day (for example, classical composers).

Other trial-and-error processes can be seen in the work of some of the most revered painters of our recent past. The talented and prolific Henri Matisse was a hugely influential artist in the 20th century. In 1935, he painted Large Reclining Nude, which is most commonly referred to as Pink Nude. What made this particular painting unique is he documented each stage of the process by taking 22 photographs over a period of 6 months. It was a complex piece that indicated the need to constantly try new approaches to get the wanted result. This painstaking method clearly showed a real-world trial-and-error process. Today, this piece is one of his most celebrated. If you have Internet access, you can easily view these 22 pictures. They are available online on the website of the Jewish Museum [4].

There are numerous similarities between the previous examples and software requirements discovery. In each case, they rely on trial-and-error procedures. This problem-solving approach enables you to find what works and eliminate what doesn't. Deliberate discovery does not happen from the failure itself but rather from understanding the failure, making an improvement, and then trying again.

Trial and error is particularly relevant in the context of software requirements. But there is a nuance to consider. Each trial is predominantly used to identify nonoptimal variations among the requirements and select what has the most potential. Feedback from stakeholders is utilized to improve results and promote deliberate discovery. Eliminating errors then becomes a process of removing what is considered by stakeholders to be inadequate and no longer a requirement.

Using Short Feedback Loops

To achieve deliberate discovery, agile frameworks such as Scrum strive for a rigorous trial-and-error process. They constantly inspect and adapt the software to the stakeholders' specifications through short feedback loops. Frequent feedback loops provide you with the ability to correct errors while costs are minimal. It is the responsibility of the team not only to learn about the problem but also to help stakeholders understand what is being built for them. In terms of requirements, this entails early and recurrent feedback loops.

In the Scrum framework a feedback loop is a *sprint*. As shown in Figure 3.1, a sprint is a time-box iteration during which a product increment is created.

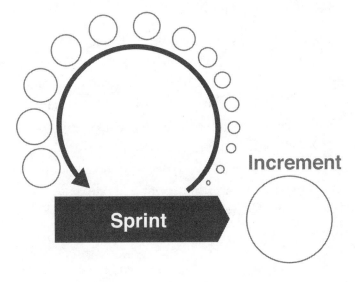

Figure 3.1 *Sprint.*

Sprints have consistent durations of one calendar month (or less). They pace the cadence at which requirements are inspected. A new sprint starts immediately after the conclusion of the previous sprint. The feedback loops caused by the sprint enable the team to adapt to the stakeholders' changing desires.

The best feedback comes from inspecting and adapting the running software with stakeholders. During each sprint, the team builds functionalities that provide value to stakeholders. It then delivers them in the form of an iteration that works. Running software is the primary mechanism used to help discover the desirable outcome. Sprints facilitate conversations between the development team and the stakeholders, creating a better understanding of the latter's perceptions. There is a powerful and important feedback loop that occurs when stakeholders have early access to running software. They can experiment with real software, come up with new ideas, and change their minds about old ideas and perceptions.

Feedback Loop and Release

Many development teams deliver software using a release, which is a combination of sprints. In the author's opinion, a release should deliver the output of only one sprint. Unfortunately, in some organizations there is a distinction between the two because many restrictions keep them from deploying software at the pace required by the sprint. As a result, only the release delivers software that works. In this case, you are left with two types of feedback loops: release and sprint. Differentiating between sprint and release is not desirable because it degrades the capacity to embrace change. Stakeholders do not have access to the monthly sprints produced by the development team.

Targeting Feedback Along the Expected Benefits

Even before starting the first sprint, as mentioned in Chapter 2, "Relying on a Stable Foundation," it is essential to have a well-established product vision. Feedback loops should align with the vision and help to share it. Clarifying why you require feedback is important. To achieve this objective, you must clearly state what feedback you expect from a sprint and make sure it fits into the overall vision of the software.

Using the expected benefits as a guide, it is worth taking the time to properly name each sprint and accurately identify its rationale. Sprints that have meaningful names make it easy for both stakeholders and the team to identify the road ahead. A set of clearly defined feedback loops should put the stakeholders at ease about the process. The team should never require blind trust from the stakeholders.

Anticipated benefits help to divide the entire scope of the software into a set of sprints, as well as prioritize them. An often-overlooked fact about prioritization is that priority is always determined in the context of criticality, and the expected benefits are a good measure of criticality. By clearly establishing what the expectations are, the importance of the benefits determines the sequencing of the sprints.

Focusing on the Stakeholders' Desirements

As mentioned in Chapter 2, software is built to solve problems. Describing those problems is the core of what constitutes the specifications. The most useful definition of the term "problem" I have ever encountered is from Gerald Weinberg and Don Gauss' book *Are Your Lights On?* [5]:

> "Problem: A difference between things as desired and things as perceived."

By this definition, software exists to satisfy unfulfilled desires. There can be no software without desires. A *desire* is a discrete piece of demonstrable functionality that is valuable to a stakeholder or a group of stakeholders. But desires alone are not the only motivation to justify the needs.

Weinberg and Gauss highlight the tension between desires and perceptions. *Perceptions* define what are required. This tension is well expressed by the neologism *desirement*, which is a blend of the words "desire" and "requirement." Desirement is "a desire so important that it is perceived as a requirement." This coined term came first from David Starr [6] who defined desirement as "a noncompiled request for software to change." [7]

Fulfilling desirements through early and continuous delivery of valuable software can result in sprints that stakeholders want to evaluate. By evaluating running software on a recurring basis, their perceptions and desires will change as much as their requests for software to change.

Unless you are both the builder and the unique user, communicating desirements is a challenging task. To have a better understanding of the challenge, picture the communication between builders and stakeholders as a large room, swathed in darkness. As there is no light, no knowledge is gleaned from the situation. To be blunt, the builders are in the dark. The stakeholders are in the room with the product owner, and they are each describing what they want. Because the product owner can hardly see, he has to rely on sound at first; and what he hears is a cacophony of dissident voices. Furthermore, imagine that the voice of each stakeholder emits a color when speaking.

As the stakeholders make their voices heard, different colors brighten the darkness. One person may emit a point of green light, another a yellow light or a red light and so on until you have a multitude of colors surrounding the product owner, like multicolored fireflies. All these lights surround him, but he is still in the dark because nothing seems to make sense.

As the product owner tries to decipher the multitude of colors lighting up the room, he will steer the conversation by asking the stakeholders what their desirements are. Then he will hone in on the responses, keeping track of when the same desirement is repeated three or four times by different stakeholders. When the key desirements start to add up, the varying colors merge, thereby creating white lights of concurrence. These white lights are a starting point from which to proceed. It is only with this basic set of common elements that the team can begin to see what the expected benefits are.

By gathering these bits of combined desirements, the team can then start building a valuable software increment and request feedback. The feedback may be successful, or there may be several stakeholders who believe their desirements were misinterpreted. By having such feedback loops, desirements are more clearly defined, and the product owner can then glean more information from the stakeholders, thereby creating better software. Feedback loops occur every few weeks and, at the end of the process, an increment is delivered to the stakeholders. After that increment is completed, this iterative process starts all over again. During the course of reaching consensus among the stakeholders, the white lights become brighter and more plentiful. The goal, for the builders, is to get to a point where the room is nearly fully lit.

With agile software development, you tackle uncertainties by trawling desirements through an iterative approach. Desirements are engaging; they enable conversations about how to create value. By shifting the focus from talking about the attributes of the solution to stakeholder's desirements, it leads to much more valuable conversations.

Summary

This chapter discussed the value of applying a trial-and-error method to tackle uncertainties and how it is particularly relevant in the context of software requirements.

Agile frameworks such as Scrum strive for a rigorous trial-and-error process. This deliberate discovery enables the team to inspect and adapt to the evolving requirements, thereby clarifying the unknowns through short feedback loops. A feedback loop enables conversations with stakeholders about their desirements, making the building of the software more transparent and efficient. A desirement is a discrete piece of demonstrable functionality that stakeholders desire and perceive as a requirement.

In the next chapter, you will learn how to express desirements and how to organize them so that you can plan the sprints.

References

[1] http://en.wikipedia.org/wiki/God_complex

[2] http://www.ted.com/talks/tim_harford.html

[3] http://lowendmac.com/orchard/05/origin-of-the-ipod.html

[4] http://thejewishmuseum.org/site/pages/uploaded_media/cone/matisse/index.html

[5] Gause, Donald C., Gerald M. Weinberg, (1990). *Are Your Lights On?* New York, NY: Dorset House Publishing.

[6] http://elegantcode.com/about/david-starr/

[7] http://visualstudiomagazine.com/articles/2013/01/07/leveling-up-agile-requirements.aspx

Chapter 4

Expressing Desirements with User Stories

You learned in the previous chapter that software comes to life by addressing desirements. The purpose of this chapter is to learn how to express and record desirements.

In this chapter, you learn about user stories, one of the most efficient techniques for identifying and discovering stakeholders' desirements. This chapter discusses decoupling roles, desires, and benefits to establish a ubiquitous language and enforce a shared understanding. It concludes by explaining that a product backlog should be used to record the user stories.

Describing Desirements by Using User Stories

People interact with software to satisfy their desires. Their most important desires become requirements or, in other words, their desirements. When the focus is on identifying stakeholders' desirements, user stories are one of the most efficient techniques. A user story is a short description written in everyday language that represents a discrete piece of demonstrable functionality. It is a desirable outcome benefitting the stakeholder. Mike Cohn, in his book *User Stories Applied* [1] defines a user story as the following:

"A user story describes functionality that will be valuable to either a user or purchaser of a system or software."

A user story is a placeholder containing just enough information so that the stakeholders can rank it and the team can produce a reasonable estimate of the effort it will take to implement it. An effective user story, which the team can plan in a sprint, shouldn't take more than a few days to implement.

A user story should be free of technical jargon; it needs to be comprehensible to both developers and stakeholders. A user story should be written as a one-liner using the classic template recommended by Mike Cohn:

As a <role>, I want <desire> so that <benefit>.

The core of the story is the "I want <desire>" section. The desire describes an activity done by a stakeholder. A stakeholder is a person who performs a role to satisfy his desire and obtain benefits. When describing a desire, it helps to indicate how it will be used rather than how it might look or how it might be implemented. Look for desires that start with or include an action verb. Here are examples of user stories for the "MTA Self-Serve Smartcard Ticketing Kiosk" software:

As a <student>, I want <to buy a pass valid only on school days> so that I can <go to school>.

The template for user stories helps to answer the classic "Who," "What," "Why" questions:

Who = role

What = desire

Why = benefit

User stories are a quick way of documenting a stakeholder's desirable outcome without being bogged down by the writing of detailed requirements specification. They encourage the team to defer collecting details.

An initial high-level story can be written as a first draft and then split into more stories when the team refines the software. Although user stories are not formally recognized as a Scrum practice, more and more teams are adopting this technique for expressing desirements.

A well-written user story follows the INVEST mnemonic developed by Bill Wake [2]. It fulfills the criteria of Independent, Negotiable, Valuable, Estimable, Small, and Testable. Here's what each criterion means:

- **Independent:** A story should stand alone and be self-contained without depending on other stories.

- **Negotiable:** A story is a placeholder that facilitates conversation and negotiation between the team and stakeholders. At any time, the story can be rewritten or even discarded. A story is not fixed and set in stone, up until it is part of the upcoming sprint.

- **Valuable:** A story needs to deliver value to the stakeholders (either the end user or the purchaser).

- **Estimable:** The team needs to be able to roughly estimate the size of the effort to complete the story.

- **Small:** A story can start its life as a big placeholder. As time goes by and you better understand the intricacies of the desires, the placeholder will be split into smaller stories. When the most important ones are close to being delivered, they need to be small enough so that they can be completed in a single sprint.

- **Testable:** A story must provide the necessary information to clearly define the acceptance criteria that confirm the story is completed.

Although the core of the story is the one-liner that sums up the desire, the most important part is invisible. User stories encourage a process whereby software is iteratively refined based on conversation and confirmation between stakeholders and the team. The details are worked out in the conversation, and the success criteria are recorded in the confirmation.

Now, with the advent of computer-based tools, user story descriptions are stored as electronic items, but traditionally, the descriptions were hand-written on paper note cards. This is why in the early days of agile software development "Card, Conversation, and Confirmation" were considered the three essential aspects of user stories. Ron Jeffries [3] wrote a famous article on these three aspects. They later became known as "the three Cs of user stories."

Discovering Desirements by Exploring Roles and Benefits

Specifying the requirements from a single perspective does not reflect the experiences, backgrounds, and desirements of every stakeholder. While writing stories, it is important to identify all the stakeholder roles that the software must absolutely and positively satisfy. It is unusual that stakeholders come down to a single role. This is why the template for user stories begins with the section "As a <role>, I want ...." It reminds us that there are several types of stakeholders.

A role is a collection of stakeholders pursuing the same desires while interacting with the software. A single stakeholder can fulfill more than one role. Whenever possible, stick with roles that define people as opposed to systems. However, consider a nonhuman role if you think that it may make or break the success of the software.

A role must have a unique name that differentiates it and sets it apart from others, especially when it is read in user stories. For example, student, tourist, and worker are all good candidate stakeholder roles for "MTA Self-Serve Smartcard Ticketing Kiosk" software:

> As a **<student>**, I want ...
>
> As a **<tourist>**, I want ...
>
> As a **<worker>**, I want ...

In addition to retrieving the names of roles in the stories, some teams may feel the need to specifically record stakeholder roles with a short description. Any useful information that helps distinguish one role from another can be part of the written description. However, the aim of role modeling is not so much to create personas but to discover missing stories. By sorting stories by role, the missing desires for each stakeholder are highlighted.

> As a <student>, I want <to buy a pass valid only on school days> so that I can <go to school>.
>
> As a <student>, I want <to buy a monthly pass> so that I can <go to school and get around>.
>
> As a <tourist>, I want <to buy a daily pass> so that I can <visit the city for one day>.
>
> As a <tourist>, I want <to buy a multiple day pass> so that I can <visit the city for more than one day>.
>
> As a <worker>, I want <to buy a monthly pass> so that I can <go to work>.

It should be noted that even if the desire <to buy a monthly pass> is the same for the worker and the student, it is important not to consolidate the story into one. The benefit sought is probably not the same because the role is not equivalent. Usually, each role expects a specific behavior and requires a different experience.

Similarly, another technique for discovering missing stories is to focus on the expected benefits. Rather than promoting the roles, use a different template for writing a user story, moving <benefit> forward in the phrase to emphasize it:

In order to <benefit>, as a <role> I want <desire>.

Sorting user stories by benefit can help you easily discover if there are missing desires:

> In order to <go to school>, as a <student> I want <to buy a pass valid only on school days>.
>
> In order to <go to school and get around> as a <student>, I want <to buy a monthly pass>.
>
> In order to <visit the city for one day> as a <tourist>, I want <to buy a daily pass>.
>
> In order to <visit the city for more than one day>, as a <tourist> I want <to buy a multiple day pass>.

Establishing a Ubiquitous Language

Eric Evans, in the book *Domain-Driven Design*, defines a ubiquitous language as a language structured around the domain model and used by all team members to connect all the activities of the team with the software [4]. Both of the templates previously described simplify conversations with stakeholders and are efficient ways of establishing a ubiquitous language. By decoupling roles, desires, and benefits, it creates, in a given context, a vocabulary that describes selected aspects of the problem to solve.

A user story fundamentally restrains conversations so that a creative collaboration between the team and stakeholders can occur. By engaging in this type of methodical discussion, both parties can iteratively cut closer to the conceptual heart of the problem. This ubiquitous language makes more explicit the tacit knowledge of "What" will be built. It ensures the building of the right "thing" before building the "thing" right.

With the emergence of powerful computer-based tools, the team can easily discover the incongruities, inconsistencies, and similarities in the vocabulary of the problem domain. With the appropriate software tool, a single mouse click enables the sorting or grouping by role, desire, or benefit.

Recording Desirements by Using a Product Backlog

While identifying stakeholders' desirements, it is important to record them in a product backlog. The product backlog is a list where the accumulation of user stories is recorded. This ordered list aggregates all potential desirements and ranks them by the perceived value. As shown in Figure 4.1, the product backlog is therefore the "What" that will be built, sorted by importance.

Order	As a/an...	I want to...	So That...	Size
1	. . .	. . .	. . .	. . .
2	. . .	. . .	. . .	. . .
3	. . .	. . .	. . .	. . .
4	. . .	. . .	. . .	. . .

Figure 4.1 *Product backlog is the list of desirements sorted by importance.*

If your organization is migrating to Scrum, you surely have many kinds of requirements scattered here and there, such as bug reports, support tickets, change requests, or use cases. These requirements should not be ignored. However, you must merge them in the product backlog so that there is a unique source of truth for expressing desirements.

An important property in the product backlog is the size of each item. When dealing with emerging needs, it is impossible to fill the entire backlog with perfect user stories, all small in size. Only the top elements need to be perfect.

The product backlog is not a static object; it is a dynamic entity. The list of user stories evolves over time. New stories are usually poorly defined and quite large, which is acceptable because they have a low priority. They are placeholders that lie at the bottom of the product backlog.

As you move forward, you actively groom user stories by moving them up on the backlog. By the time they move up in the current sprint, refinement splits large stories into simpler units that the development team can build. Themes of stories emerge and this helps the product owner combine the stories into meaningful sets for sprinting.

Mike Cohn presents this grooming process as the product backlog iceberg [5]. He suggests that we think of the product backlog as an iceberg. At the top are small stories that are ready for a team to implement in the current sprint. At the bottom of the iceberg are larger stories that may take many weeks or perhaps months to build, if not refine. While the team works on a set of functionalities in the current sprint, the iceberg melts, new stories rise to the surface, and the iceberg gets smaller. In this process, "ready to sprint" stories emerge, just enough and just in time. Inspired by the iceberg-like shape, Figure 4.2 presents a more realistic vision of what a product backlog is.

Is It Normal to Record Bugs in the Backlog?

When people report a bug, the general consensus tends to be that it consists of a mistake or failure in the software. Definitions of bugs abound and the words *flaw*, *error*, or *fault* often comes up. When individuals use software, they may encounter problems. Perhaps they cannot utilize the software the way it was expected. Perhaps, as well, the elements developers claimed to have included don't work in the way they described. Both of these examples are real bugs that need to be fixed in the current sprint.

Often when someone describes something as a bug, it is a desirement and not a bug. The complaints should be interpreted as a request for software to change. This constitutes a large percentage of reported bugs. In such cases, the team should not fix the bug in the current sprint but, instead, treat it like a user story and insert it in the backlog for prioritization.

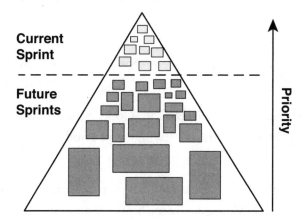

Figure 4.2 *Product backlog is like an iceberg.*

The product backlog not only enables stakeholders to establish a vision, but also to decide what desirements the team should address during the next sprint. By making desirements visible and explicit, the product backlog ensures a shared understanding. By clearly setting the priorities, it is much easier for the team responsible for "How" the software will be built to plan and monitor its work.

Summary

This chapter explained how to express the stakeholders' desirements with user stories. A user story is a short description written in everyday language using the classic template: "As a <role>, I want <desire> so that <benefit>." By decoupling roles, desires, and benefits, user stories establish a ubiquitous language that enforces a shared understanding.

This chapter concluded with a presentation of the product backlog. The product backlog is an ordered list where the accumulation of user stories is recorded. The product backlog not only helps to organize the user stories, but also to communicate them to the team. It is a key element of executable specifications. Therefore, the next chapter is dedicated solely to the product backlog.

References

[1] Cohn, Mike (2004). *User Stories Applied: For Agile Software Development*. Boston, MA: Addison-Wesley.

[2] Wake, Bill (2003, August 17). "INVEST in Good Stories, and SMART Tasks". http://xp123.com/articles/invest-in-good-stories-and-smart-tasks/

[3] Jeffries, Ron (2001, August 30). "Essential XP: Card, Conversation, and Confirmation". *XP Magazine*. http://xprogramming.com/articles/expcardconversationconfirmation/

[4] Evans, Eric (2003). *Domain Driven Design*. Boston, MA: Addison-Wesley.

[5] Cohn, Mike (2009). *Succeeding with Agile: Software Development Using Scrum*. Boston, MA: Addison-Wesley.

Chapter 5

Refining User Stories by Grooming the Product Backlog

You learned in the previous chapter that iterative discovery of desirements involves expressing user stories with the help of a product backlog. The purpose of this chapter is to learn how to groom the product backlog so that you can plan sprints that will increase the quality of feedback loops.

In this chapter, you will learn the importance of the product owner for the product backlog. This chapter discusses how the team refines user stories by grooming the product backlog. Grooming is the act of ranking, illustrating, sizing, and splitting user stories. You will see how to use collaboration boards to make explicit the grooming process, with a minimum of formality. Finally, it concludes by explaining how to organize effective sprints with story mapping.

Managing the Product Backlog

Nowadays, it is unlikely that new software must address the needs of a single stakeholder. On average, there are easily between 10 and 20 stakeholders. This requires the involvement of several people. If the product backlog is an ordered list, and the stakeholders are responsible for setting the priority, how do you ensure the list actually gets sorted and that every item does not end up being poorly defined? Assigning the product backlog ownership to a group of people is not a viable solution. Scrum recognizes this issue by defining a specific role for this responsibility, the product owner.

The product owner is responsible for ensuring that the product backlog is always in a healthy state. He is the primary interface between the development team and the stakeholders. The product owner is the definitive authority on all that concerns requirements. His main responsibility is to decide the ordering of what will be built and list these decisions into the product backlog.

One of the primary qualities of the product owner is to be the bearer of the vision. He understands the big picture. This knowledge gives that person the authority to prioritize the importance of the desirements expressed by stakeholders. Faced with the unexpected, the product owner knows how to stay the course and is responsive to the stakeholders' changes.

There is a lot of responsibility (both explicit and implicit) involved in managing the product backlog. Work will not get done without someone actively collaborating with stakeholders to understand customer/market needs and then communicating with the development team to ensure those needs are met. Being the product owner does not mean that he decides alone. The development team actively takes a hand in backlog management.

Is the Product Owner the New Role for Analysts?

Within an agile framework, creating a new user story is an activity open to all. It can be done either by a stakeholder or by a team member. It is strongly recommended that stakeholders write the stories without requiring business analysts to act as a proxy between them and the team. There are cases in which the product owner creates a story in response to a request from stakeholders, but this scenario is not mandatory.

Because of her experience and know-how, there are similarities between the analyst and product owner roles. However, they are two different roles in the Scrum team. There is a major difference between a true analyst and a product owner. Product owners represent the business and have the authority to make decisions that affect their product. Typically, an analyst does not have this decision-making authority.

To have a true business analyst step into the role of product owner is possible but not always the best option. For example, here is a scenario in which a business analyst is probably not the best choice for owning and maintaining the product backlog. Say you are an independent software vendor selling software to thousands of users. In this case, someone must focus on both the customer and market, adapting the iteration plan and evolving the product roadmap. An analyst is not trained for that job.

You must realize that the evolving role of the analyst does not necessarily consist of being a product owner. Someone else with stronger marketing skills than the business analyst could also inherit this responsibility. In the next chapter, you will learn that, by default, the role of the analyst is now more tactical. He handles a myriad of details and still does analysis, but now mostly focuses inward on the delivery team.

This new, strategic role is more than just *backlog prioritization*. It is about facilitating software development over successive sprints and ensuring appropriate customer/market needs are inserted into that process.

Though this role is typically assigned to someone with technical background, someone from marketing or product management is probably just as qualified. If any of these people cannot fulfill the role, someone with a solid understanding of end users, the marketplace, the competition, or future trends can become the product owner. This is not a solitary role—the product owner is most likely part of a larger team—perhaps in product management (if an independent software vendor) or in a client-facing team (if in consulting).

Collaborating to Groom the Product Backlog

When dealing with emerging needs, it is impossible to keep the entire backlog in a ready state; only the top elements need to be. A healthy backlog provides a set of high-value, ready desirements, about equal in size, that are small enough so that the team can deliver them in the upcoming sprints. To obtain desirements that are ready to iterate, you need to periodically groom the backlog.

Even with all the improvements wrought by the Scrum framework, grooming the backlog remains, and likely will remain, a fundamentally human endeavor, fueled by the insights, ideas, passions, and perceptions of people looking for the best. Rather than letting stakeholders work of their own free will, the product owner must lead everyone by using a sequence of activities that promotes deliberate discovery. Grooming the backlog boils down to a sequence of four activities: ranking, illustrating, sizing, and splitting user stories, as shown in Figure 5.1.

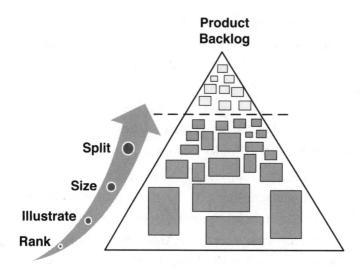

Figure 5.1 *Grooming the backlog.*

These activities are never performed solo by the product owner. To accomplish these activities, the product owner must collaborate: first with stakeholders and then with the development team. Backlog grooming is a team effort.

Ranking User Stories with a Dot Voting Method

Although, according to the development team, the product owner is perceived as the one who decides the ordering of the backlog, it is actually not his decision. He must rely on stakeholders who are the ones who decide the importance of each story.

For the product owner, ranking user stories is actually a contact sport with stakeholders. It requires that he brings all his senses to the task and applies the best of his thinking, his feelings, and his communication skills to the challenge of facilitating decision making. The product owner is a facilitator, not a decider. Because he understands the process of grooming the backlog, he can guide stakeholders.

As mentioned in Chapter 3, "Discovering Through Short Feedback Loops and Stakeholders' Desirements," you can picture the communication between builders and stakeholders as a large room swathed in darkness. The product owner is in the room having conversations with stakeholders and what he hears is a cacophony of dissident voices. Because there is no light, little knowledge is derived from the situation. Now, imagine that the voice of each stakeholder emits a color when speaking.

The product owner steers the conversation by asking stakeholders what is the most important desirement. Soon, he will be surrounded with multicolored fireflies representing stakeholders' desirements. By forcing the writing of the desirements as a user story, this can simplify the answers and increase the likelihood that the same desirement can repeated by several stakeholders. When user stories begin to accumulate, all the different colors merge, creating sparkling white lights. Order springs from the cacophony. These white lights are the important stories, those that the product owner must rank at the top of the backlog.

So far, the ranking process as described may seem abstract. Forget the abstract to be more practical. Usually, when discussing ranking, authors prefer to present the most common techniques, such as binary search tree, Kano analysis, MoSCoW (Must-Should-Could-Would), or other numeral assignment techniques. Now do the same by using one of the preferred methods: the dot voting technique (also known as spending your dollar technique). This established facilitation method is widely used by workshop facilitators for prioritizing ideas among a large number of people, and for deciding which are the most important to take forward.

The method is summarized as follows:

1. Post the user stories on the wall using yellow stickies or in some manner that enables each item to receive votes.

2. Give four to five dots to each stakeholder.

3. Ask the stakeholders to place their votes. Stakeholders should apply dots (using pens, markers, or, most commonly, stickers) under or beside written stories to show which ones they prefer.

4. Order the product backlog from the most number of dots to the least.

When you are done with this first pass, it is almost certain that the stakeholders will not be completely happy with the outcome of the vote. If that is the case, you should review the voting and optimize it. Here's what you can do:

1. Arrange the votes into three groups to represent high, medium, and low priorities.

2. Discuss stories in each group.

3. Move items around to create a high-priority list.

4. Make a new vote with items in the high-priority list.

The goal during this review is to start a discussion about each group. Discuss which user stories are a low or medium priority, and which must be delivered in the near future. Why are they low priority? After discussion, stakeholders may agree to move them into the high-priority list. Also, discuss the stories that are almost high priority and decide if you should move them in the high-priority list. When you are done with the discussion, repeat voting, this time using only the items that belong to the high-priority list. Finish this second vote by ordering the product backlog from the most number of dots to the least.

Identifying the user stories that are top priorities is the first step of a two-step process. The second step is to ensure that the stories are small enough so that the team can build them in a sprint. To achieve this goal, the product owner must shift focus and start discussions with the development team. Unlike stakeholders, the team members are the ones who can measure the size of user stories.

Sizing requires a rough understanding by the development team of the user experience. The user experience enables stakeholders to discuss the success criteria. These criteria say in the words of the stakeholders how they expect the software to behave.

During this second step, seek to quickly define success criteria, so the team estimates the size of stories as soon as possible and with minimum effort. A storyboard is the perfect medium for achieving this goal. If user stories help monitor conversations with stakeholders, storyboards help to illustrate expectations rapidly and cheaply. They are concrete examples that provide the explicit information required by the development team.

Illustrating User Stories with Storyboards

As experience teaches, stakeholders love to envision the software from the user interface standpoint. As a result, often they specify how the software should work, rather than just what it is supposed to do. This is why illustrating user stories with a storyboard is so efficient.

Storyboards, as we know them today, were developed at the Walt Disney Studios in the 1930s. The first storyboards evolved from comic book-like story sketches. They were used to "preview" an animation before a single animated cartoon was produced.

Figure 5.2 shows an example of a storyboard for an animated film. Not only does a storyboard make possible a dress rehearsal of the final product, but also by posting it on the wall, it elicits early feedback and encourages quick, painless editing, leading to significant savings in time and resources.

Figure 5.2 *An example of a storyboard for an animated film.*

For the general public, a storyboard means drawing pre-production pictures for video production, animation, and film making. Unfortunately, too few know that storyboarding also applies to software development. It helps to illustrate the important steps of the user experience.

It is tough to capture the big picture without visually depicting the user story. Explaining requirements from the perspective of the user interface helps to turn unspoken assumptions into explicit information. In addition, explicit information helps stakeholders think and communicate effectively. To keep up a healthy conversation between stakeholders, the product owner, and the development team, each user story should be enhanced with a storyboard. During specifications, the screens required to illustrate the user story are roughly sketched, either on paper or through the use of computer-based software.

Do not expect the storyboard to be a visual prototype that looks like the final user interface. It is an artistic rendition in which many details are missing. A storyboard is a low-fidelity visual aid that communicates the visible behaviors of a user story.

The process of visual thinking enables stakeholders and the product owner to brainstorm together, placing their ideas on storyboards and then arranging them in a structured way. This fosters more ideas and generates consensus within the group. The reason for the usefulness of a storyboard is that it helps stakeholders, as well as the development team, understand exactly how the user story will work. It is also more cost-effective to make changes to a storyboard than to an implemented user story.

The simplest technique for creating storyboards is *paper prototyping* [1]. It involves creating rough, even hand-sketched, drawings of the user interface to use as throwaway prototypes. All interactions within the prototype are simulated. Although paper prototyping is sketchy and incomplete, this simple method of communication with stakeholders can provide a great deal of useful feedback that can result in the design of better user stories. Figure 5.3 demonstrates how you can easily sketch ideas, test them almost instantaneously with stakeholders, and get rapid feedback on what does and does not work.

Figure 5.3 *An example of a paper prototype.*

After collecting and visualizing ideas on how the user interface might look, when there is a consensus on the user experience, it is desirable to keep an electronic copy of the storyboard for future reference. The simplest technique is to transform the paper prototype into a low-fidelity computer-based storyboard. The storyboard can then be used as a visual illustration of the user story, which will be shared with the development team. It is important, however, to make sure that you do not use a software tool that attempts to make the user interface similar to the final product. These high-fidelity tools encourage precision, and specifying all the details is time-consuming and deemed inappropriate at this time.

Figure 5.4 shows a low-fidelity computerized storyboard for the following user story, "As a student, I want to select a transit fare so that I can buy it."

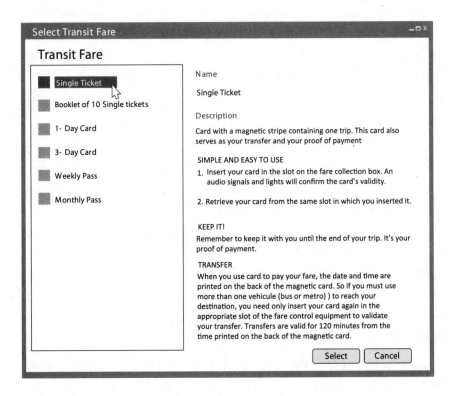

Figure 5.4 *A computerized low-fidelity storyboard.*

Designing the storyboards is always the responsibility of the product owner. He may nonetheless be assisted by the team members while performing his duties. For example, business analysts can help to complete the computerized storyboards. However, this activity is essential for obtaining a healthy backlog, and the product owner must be fully involved.

Sizing User Stories Using Comparison

The biggest and most common problem product owners encounter is stories that are too big. If a story is too big and overly complex while being a top priority, the sprint is at risk of not being properly completed. To avoid this issue, product owners must identify, as early as possible, if a user story is the right size and therefore ready to be built during a sprint.

It is not the responsibility of the product owner to estimate the work that needs to be done to complete each story. Only the development team can identify the size of a story. After the development team makes those estimates, the product owner can then determine if the story is too big. If that is the case, with the help of the team, she will split it into smaller stories.

To estimate the size of the top stories in the backlog, the product owner must organize recurring backlog grooming meetings. All the members of the development team must attend these meetings. To answer any questions addressed during these meetings, subject matter experts (stakeholders) should also participate. Before the meeting occurs, the product owner prioritizes the story list, thereby ensuring the most important stories will be estimated. The meeting is then time-boxed, at usually one hour, and each story is considered. Don't worry if you don't have time to discuss all the stories in the backlog. They will be addressed in future meetings.

Sizing a story requires that the development team estimates the work to be done to complete it. This should be simple, but unfortunately human beings are not good at estimating. Actually, we are not good at all.

Cognitive scientists tell us that our brain is wired to imagine the possible. We are reluctant to identify limitations, especially if they are not obvious. It seems that we are too optimistic, and indeed, we would not have survived the evolution of our species without this trait. With this bias built into our genetic background, it is almost impossible for us to accurately estimate, at least in a short time. It is obvious that with a lot of resources and enough time, humans just get there. However, this is not our case as we seek to estimate a user story in less than 5 minutes.

Does this mean that the development team should not estimate? Yes, at least according to what the word "estimate" means today. I propose that you estimate differently. Stop measuring absolute values and start comparing relative values. When estimating, you should not measure effort but instead compare efforts using a reference point.

Humans are poor at estimating absolute sizes. However, we are great at assessing relative sizes. For example, imagine that a team must estimate the weight of a young child and an adult. It will be difficult to agree on the exact weight of each. However, it will be extremely easy to decide which one is heavier.

When you measure stories, you need to be concerned with only relative sizes. You can easily do this by using the Fibonacci sequence or series, which is "A sequence of numbers, such as 1, 1, 2, 3, 5, 8, 13..., in which each successive number is equal to the sum of the two preceding numbers". What is of interest, in this sequence, is the ratio between any number and its counterpart. This series gives you a relative size you can work with to compare effectively.

Our cultural tendency is to estimate based on how many hours it will take to complete a story. Unfortunately, estimating using duration reduces the team to measuring absolute values, which is what we want to avoid. Because of our incapacity to anticipate the unknown and to predict risk, we should steer clear of estimating based on time. There are three reasons for this:

- The time necessary for teams to build one unit of work fluctuates from sprint to sprint. In a complex situation, there is no other choice than to work collaboratively. When a member of the team is absent, due to vacation periods or members leaving the team, the team's capacity to deliver changes. As a result, if you measure effort based on the number of hours, you must perpetually revisit the estimates in the backlog.

- Estimating based on time requires you to take into account the slack time. This adds accidental complexity, which results in a more imprecise measure. Factoring slack time appropriately is difficult. You must take into consideration the fact that people have to check their emails, participate in other meetings, eat lunch, take breaks throughout the day, and so on.

- Each team will gauge risks differently. Some will plan for a large cushion of time to mitigate risk, whereas others will approach the challenge without compensation.

The best way to evaluate effort is to use a degree of difficulty summarizing numerically the effort, complexity, and risk. For every degree of difficulty, you will assign points. Story points are independent of variations engendered by units of time. Furthermore, they are the perfect unit for comparing relative values.

The challenge of using a points system is calibrating what the number of points means. Some team members may think a story is worth one point, whereas others may think it is worth 10 points. So, how do you solve such a problem? One of the ways of calibrating stories, and getting a joint agreement by all team members, is to look at previous examples of stories as a referential. The team ranks the stories from most difficult to least difficult. The most difficult will have more story points than the least difficult. The goal is to end up with representative stories of 1, 2, 3, 5, 8, 13, and 20 points. After those representative stories have been identified, the team can then decide how many points the new stories should be awarded. Calibrating by story points enables a team to easily reach a consensus.

During backlog grooming meetings, you want insights from all team members. As a result, you should favor a consensus-based estimation technique. A well-known and effective technique is the planning poker technique. It was first introduced by James Grenning and later popularized by Mike Cohn in his book, *Agile Estimating and Planning* [3].

Approach this technique as though you were playing a game of poker. Each bet should target one story. Before each bet, the product owner presents a short overview of the story and demonstrates the storyboard to define the success criteria needed to finish it. While answering questions posed by team members, the product owner enhances these criteria, which could double or even triple the work needed for each story. When the question period is over, the Scrum master then chairs the meeting and gives each team member a deck of Fibonacci cards, as shown in Figure 5.5.

Figure 5.5 *Deck of Fibonacci cards.*

The idea is to have all participants use one of the Fibonacci cards to give a rough estimate of how many points she thinks a story is worth. When betting, everyone turns over their card simultaneously so as not to influence others. Those who have placed high estimates, as well as those who have low estimates, are given the opportunity to justify their reasoning. After the members have explained their choices, the team bets again until a consensus is reached. This estimation period is usually time-boxed at five minutes by the Scrum master to ensure structure and efficiency. If consensus is not reached within the set time, the product owner moves to the next story where the betting process begins again. The goal is to address and reach an agreement on as many stories as possible within one meeting.

When the meeting is over, the product owner takes into consideration the number of points assigned to each story. Some stories may be worth 20 points, whereas others are worth 5 points. The product owner must determine which stories are too large and therefore need to be divided into smaller stories. Splitting large stories allows the development team to approach each smaller story in a more productive manner.

Splitting User Stories Along Business Values

Most user stories are too large; at least, this is the trend we noted with teams transitioning to agile software development. We guess this is because it is difficult to understand the gist of what a user story is. We must go back to basics and remember that it was initiated by Extreme Programming (XP). In *Planning Extreme Programming* [4] by Kent Beck and Martin Fowler, a user story is defined in the following way:

> "We demonstrate progress by delivering tested, integrated code that implements a story. A story should be understandable to customers and developers, testable, valuable to the customer and small enough so that the programmers can build half a dozen in an iteration."

A story is a short description of a unit of software that works, delivers value, and generates feedback from stakeholders.

A rule of thumb used to determine whether a story is small enough is to take the average velocity of the team per iteration and divide it by two. The velocity is the number of story points completed during a sprint. The product owner should not plan stories that are bigger than one-half the velocity.

A common mistake made when splitting stories is to slice and dice along technical issues, such as along the development process line (design, code, test, and deploy) or along the architectural line (user interface, business logic, and database). In addition to being difficult to deliver and deploy, technical decomposition creates stories that generate little feedback because they are incomprehensible by stakeholders. These stories negatively affect the iterative discovery of the stakeholders' desirements. This is not the path to follow.

You should focus on the perspective of stakeholders by thin slicing stories that favor the business value. *Thin slicing* is based on evolutionary architecture; it provides stories that implement only a small bit of functionality, but all the way through the architecture layers of the software. Thin slicing always splits stories along self-contained increments of value and along self-contained bundles of work that include "design, code, tests, and deploy." There are two usual patterns for thin slicing stories in a self-contained unit:

- **Division:** The division pattern provides smaller stories, often of equal size.

  When there are clear boundaries about operational workflow or data manipulation, our first choice is to divide along these lines. For example, if it makes sense, you should split along the workflow steps involved or split according to each variation in business rules. If this is not a successful track, try to split by the type of data the story manipulates or along create-read-update-delete (CRUD) boundaries.

- **Simplification:** The simplification pattern aims to remove what is not necessary.

- When division is not an option, you should reduce the scope of a large story by keeping only the bare minimum. This is not a popular choice with stakeholders. As always, everything seems essential, and this requires more demanding conversations. Consider applying the XP principle: Do the Simplest Thing That Could Possibly Work. Remove from the large story everything that is not indispensable. Create one or more stories to safeguard what is not essential. These non-essential stories will be placed at the bottom of the backlog, whereas the remainder and thinner story will continue its journey to the top of the backlog.

Tracking User Stories with a Collaboration Board

Backlog grooming is a team effort. Everyone, including stakeholders, must collaborate to evolve user stories from the bottom to the top of the backlog. As shown in Figure 5.6, it is a dynamic and active workflow where stories are constantly enhanced.

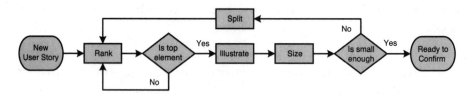

Figure 5.6 *The backlog grooming workflow.*

The team must master each step of the workflow; otherwise, the story will not progress as expected. Team members must synchronize their efforts on a daily basis. Unfortunately, the backlog is of little use to guide this work. At best, you can add a status field to follow the process, but it does not encourage collaboration. Instead, it is more efficient to use visual aids inspired by collaboration boards such as those offered through the Slingboards [5] platform.

A collaboration board communicates information by using sticky notes instead of texts or other written instructions. As shown in Figure 5.7, a collaboration board is a two-dimensional grid on which you move yellow stickies from column to column to guide the actions of team members.

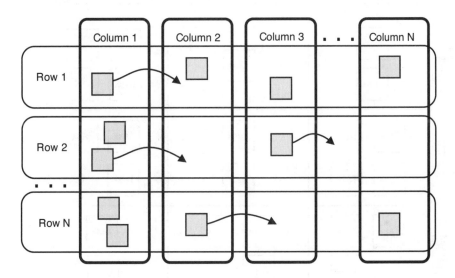

Figure 5.7 *A collaboration board is a two-dimensional grid.*

Each column represents a state of the process, and each sticky note is a visual signal for guiding the collaboration. The aim is to move each sticky note from state to state to accomplish a workflow. The rows are used to group and organize the yellow stickies in a logical manner. If you expect to have only a few stickies, you can have a single row without any grouping.

A well-known example of a collaboration board heavily used by agile teams is a task board. *A task board* is a visual aid that guides the work of a team during a sprint. As shown in Figure 5.8, a task board is a constantly evolving summary of the team's forecasts for the current sprint. It enables you to see at a glance what is done, what remains to be done, and who is working on what.

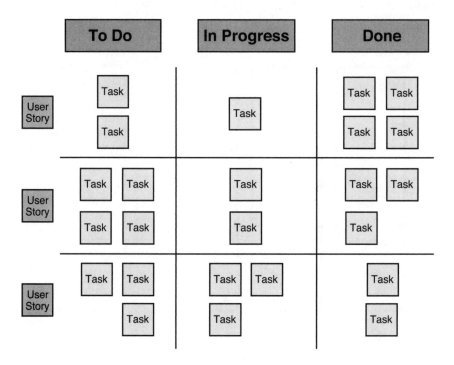

Figure 5.8 *A task board is a well-known example of a collaboration board.*

When a sticky note is moved from column to column, it serves as a signal for guiding the collaboration. More and more teams consider a task board as essential to ensuring a rich collaboration during the sprint. I believe the same is true during backlog grooming except that we must use a different collaboration board. Now see how you could create a grooming board to get the same benefits.

The most important items in a collaboration board are the columns because they make it possible to visualize the process. Several options are available to define the columns. As shown in Figure 5.9, a simple option would be to have a column for each step. A major disadvantage of this option is that you can hardly know when a step is completed. There is no visual signal to initiate collaboration between teammates.

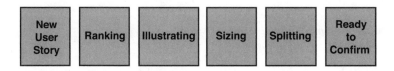

Figure 5.9 *A collaboration board with no signals.*

A second option, as shown in Figure 5.10, is to alert collaborators by being explicit when a step is done. There are two disadvantages to this approach for grooming. First, this approach assumes that the process is linear, which is not true. Grooming requires a lot of backtracking, such as when splitting a story. Second, we are uncomfortable with a condition that states that the ranking is completed. Ranking is never completely finished and can occur at any time during the grooming.

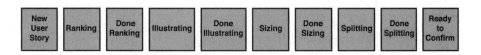

Figure 5.10 *A collaboration board with "Done" signals.*

A third option is to alert collaborators by signaling that a step is ready for processing. This is the option that you can adopt, as it applies well to the grooming process. Figure 5.11 shows what the collaboration board would look like with one row for the backlog.

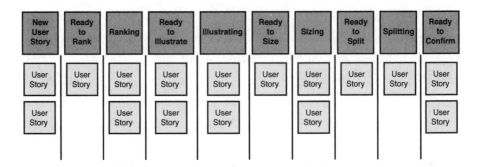

Figure 5.11 *A collaboration board with "Ready" signals.*

The contents of the sticky note, which are moved from column to column, should display relevant information to help teammates understand what is going on. Significant information improves communication and reduces interruptions. As shown in Figure 5.12, there are nine potential display areas on a collaboration sticker.

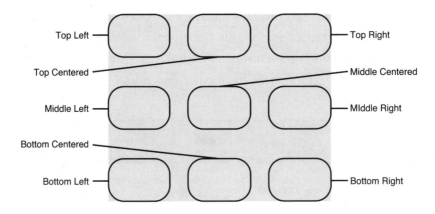

Figure 5.12 *A collaboration sticker has nine display areas.*

When we want to create a collaboration board to facilitate the grooming process, each sticky note is going to represent a user story. Figure 5.13 shows the final result for this type of sticker. Note that we have not used all display areas, only those that we considered necessary.

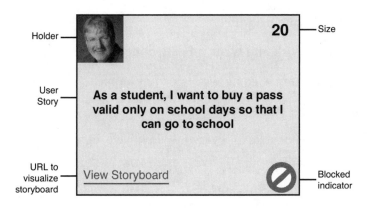

Figure 5.13 *A collaboration sticker representing a user story.*

The blocked indicator is visually pinning a status tag to the sticker. This status tag enables you to visualize work that is not directly associated with the value-added steps being performed. It creates visibility and awareness and enables the right people to react quickly to that new status. A visual alternative to pinning is creating special columns in your collaboration board that fulfill the same purpose. Although this is valid, and many people do it, we prefer pinning to expose that something is going wrong, or not happening. Board real estate is expensive. If you start creating special columns for each status a sticky note can have, you might quickly fill the board with empty zones.

A collaboration board is a clear, simple, and effective way to organize and present work during grooming. It increases the efficiency and effectiveness of the work by making visible the rules of collaboration and thus facilitating the flow. Flow is the mental state of operation in which a person performing an activity is fully immersed in a feeling of energized focus, full involvement, and enjoyment in the process of the activity.

Visual collaboration keeps the group members in the flow united around common performance measures. It enhances communication and reduces friction by making explicit the information teammates care about. It helps teammates

- Understand and indicate priorities.

- Identify the flow of work and what is being done.

- Identify when something is going wrong or not happening.

- Cut down on meetings to discuss work issues.

- Provide real-time feedback to everyone involved in the whole process.

- See whether performance criteria is met.

Collaboration boards increase accountability and positively influence the behavior and attitude of team members and stakeholders. Team members define and choose their own work instead of having work assigned to them. High-visibility and clear guidelines ensure teammates cannot hide work (or nonwork) from each other. They know that at any moment, if they want to, they can, with zero overhead and without causing any discomfort to anyone, see exactly what everybody is doing. Boards tend to expose the flow, but it is done with ground rules that people find quite reasonable. Thus, accountability is achieved in a harmonious way because it boils down to the individual responsibility of updating the board. This builds transparency among team members, which in turn builds trust.

Delivering a Coherent Set of User Stories

Unfortunately, in an iterative and empirical process, it is not because collaborative work produces high-value desirements that you necessarily get a "usable" sprint. Often, collaboration also requires prioritizing low-value desirements to obtain a coherent whole with optimal value. The use of a visual aid is essential in achieving this know-how. In this regard, over the years, experienced practitioners have acknowledged the necessity of structuring the backlog along a two-dimensional collaboration board. This way of organizing the stories to avoid half-baked incremental iterations was initially promoted by Jeff Patton [6] and is now known as *story mapping*.

Story mapping is the act of using a collaboration board to help in planning sprints and ordering the backlog. As illustrated in Figure 5.14, it combines high-value and low-value user stories in a coherent set, thereby revealing sprints that are of perceptible value to the stakeholders.

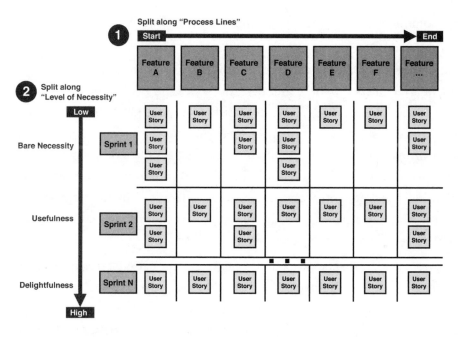

Figure 5.14 *Planning sprints with story mapping.*

The yellow stickies are the user stories from the backlog. They are distributed along the process line on the horizontal axis and simultaneously along the level of necessity on the vertical axis. Finally, they are ordered in "usable" sprints by assessing the expected necessity. Visualizing the desirements according to the process lines enables you to iteratively cut ever closer to the heart of the prioritization challenge. By doing this, you can combine the low-value functionalities and hold everything together.

As is always the case with a collaboration board, it all starts by identifying the columns. Create as many columns as there are features in the process lines. A feature is a piece of high-level functionality; a business activity that delivers value and separates into several stories. Arrange features by usage sequence, with features used early on, on the left, and later on, on the right.

Continue by creating as many rows as there are upcoming sprints. In each sprint, split stories along its feature by placing them in the appropriate column and make them overlap if they are numerous.

Even if the horizontal axis organizes stories along process lines, it does not ensure small and testable stories. Small stories should typically represent a few days of work. Initially, this is not the case as almost all new user stories are too big. They are desirements that need to be disaggregated into a set of constituent stories. Splitting desirements along the level of necessity ensures the identification of simple stories that can be forecast in a sprint. By differentiating the bare minimum necessity from usefulness and delightfulness, the product owner can divide large stories into smaller ones. These smaller stories provide immediate value and can be delivered in a sprint.

Even if desirements expressed as user stories are a starting point in understanding requirements, because they help determine the scope of work during sprints, they are mainly used as a unit of planning and delivery. This is why the overall goal of story mapping is to create a suitable scope to establish a delivery plan.

Planning Work with User Stories

There is a close link between executable specifications and agile project management. The purpose of this book is not to discuss agile project management. There are good books that cover this topic. [7] That being said, we cannot ignore that desirements provide an effective unit of planning. As shown in story mapping, we plan sprints around desirements. Actually, the strong adoption of story mapping by the agile community leads me to believe that we are not alone in thinking that agile planning is closely linked to requirements discovery.

Summary

In this chapter, you saw how to groom the product backlog by ranking, illustrating, sizing, and splitting user stories. You learned the importance of having a product owner—someone who not only leads backlog grooming, but also ensures that it is done in collaboration with stakeholders and the development team. You learned how to use collaboration boards to track user stories during the grooming process. Finally, this chapter concluded by explaining how to organize a delivery plan that provides immediate value to the stakeholders through the use of story mapping.

When a story has gone through the process of grooming, you have reached an important milestone, which is the transition from conversation to confirmation. If user stories and their storyboards help monitor conversations with stakeholders, success criteria help confirm expectations. Success criteria convey additional information about the story and establish the conditions of acceptation. They enable the team to know when it is done and they say, in the words of the stakeholders, how they expect to verify the desirable outcome. In this perspective, success criteria are a specification as important, if not more important, than the story. Success criteria are a key element of executable specifications. Therefore, the next chapter is dedicated specifically to the issue of confirming user stories.

References

[1] Snyder, Carolyn. (2003). *Paper Prototyping: The Fast and Easy Way to Design and Refine User Interfaces*. San Francisco, CA: Morgan Kaufmann.

[2] http://science.yourdictionary.com/fibonacci-sequence

[3] Cohn, Mike (2005). *Agile Estimating and Planning*. Boston, MA: Addison-Wesley.

[4] Beck, Ken, Martin Fowler (2000). *Planning Extreme Programming*. Boston, MA: Addison-Wesley.

[5] http://slingboards-lab.com

[6] Patton, Jeff (2005, January). "It's All in How You Slice It." *Better Software Magazine*. www.agileproductdesign.com/writing/how_you_slice_it.pdf

[7] Highsmith, Jim (2009). *Agile Project Management: Creating Innovative Products*. Boston, MA: Addison-Wesley.

Chapter 6

Confirming User Stories with Scenarios

The previous chapter explained that conversations enable you to tackle the uncertainty and lack of agreement between stakeholders. It demonstrated how backlog grooming is a key process in initiating these conversations. Unfortunately, whatever the quality of the conversation, few teams can confirm the desirable outcome appropriately. Words have different meanings to different people. For example, if you are asked to think of a Volkswagen, you might think of a Beetle, whereas the other person was referring to a camper van. By relying solely on user stories, this can easily lead to miscommunication between the software development team and the stakeholders. To confirm expectations without a hitch, you need to enhance the conversation with a more effective practice. The solution is to confirm user stories using concrete examples. By tying the meanings of words to concrete examples, it is much harder for people to misunderstand.

Like a mirror, there are two sides to the requirements specification. The conversation is the first side, whereas the second is confirming user stories with concrete examples. This other side of the mirror is the main theme of this chapter.

There are two categories of concrete examples that, each in their own way, serve to illustrate the expected behavior of a story:

- **Storyboard:** A rough, even hand-sketched, sequence of drawings that illustrate the important steps of the user experience for the purpose of previsualizing the behavior of a user story.

- **Scenario:** A script written in everyday language to express a specific behavior within a user story.

If user stories and their storyboards help monitor conversations with stakeholders during backlog grooming, the scenarios help to confirm expectations when the team is ready to plan a new sprint. Scenarios provide additional information about the story. This additional information enables the team to know when the story is done and says in the words of the stakeholders how they plan to verify the desirable outcome. This desirable outcome determines the success criteria. *Success criteria* establish the conditions of acceptance from the stakeholders' point of view. Scenarios are the perfect medium for expressing the success criteria.

The previous chapter explained how to illustrate user stories with storyboards. This chapter demonstrates how to confirm user stories with the help of scenarios. The core of this chapter focuses on learning how to script scenarios. By using a concise syntax, the scenario expresses a ubiquitous language, thereby creating a shared understanding. The remainder of the chapter shows you how to collaboratively confirm the scenarios using a two-step process. Finally, this chapter concludes by explaining how to evolve scenarios from sprint to sprint.

Scripting User Stories with Scenarios

Just as storyboarding is one technique for illustrating user stories, writing scripts is another equally effective way for people to determine the behavior of a story. A *script* is a sequence of instructions written in everyday language. It describes a particular scenario that is required for the fulfillment of a user story. This is an instance serving to confirm the user story. The scenario contains a precondition, an action, and a consequence. A *precondition* is the current state of the software before action is taken. An *action* is something that is accomplished to perform the behavior of the scenario. A *consequence* is the result of the action.

As shown in Figure 6.1, a *scenario* is a transition demonstrating cause and effect from the stakeholders' perspective.

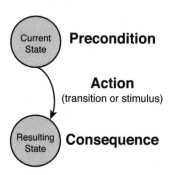

Figure 6.1 *A state transition.*

A scenario is nothing more than an action causing a state transition. The sum of all the scenarios illustrating a story makes up a conventional state machine. One of the great benefits of specifying a problem as a finite state machine is that you can complete the logic of the problem. That is, if you can enumerate the states of precondition and consequence, as well as the actions, then illustrating a user story is simply a matter of creating a transition (a scenario) for every combination. Before proceeding further, note that there should be only one action per scenario. Triggering a single action is crucial in keeping the state transition simple. Kicking off several actions creates confusion. You do not want to analyze and understand how multiple actions collaborate to produce the final consequences. If a set of actions is important from a domain perspective, it is probably important enough to be given a name by itself and used as a single state transition. For example, imagine a state transition with the following two actions:

```
Select a product
Pay for the product
```

You should replace the two actions with a single action, which in this case is more generic:

```
Buy the product
```

A scenario can use several preconditions and consequences as long as they are all directly related to the action specified by the scenario.

Expressing Scenarios with Formality

Scenarios connect the human concept of cause and effect to the software concept of input-process-output. It provides a clear and precise language to help improve communication not only with humans, but with software development tools as well. With enough formality, a tool can be written that interprets the intent of these scenarios and tests the software under construction. This ensures the specifications work as stated.

Test, Scenario, or Example?

Those who are familiar with the latest trends regarding executable specifications may ask why we use the word "scenario" instead of another name such as "example" or the overused word "test." These trends are known by many names because many disparate groups are concerned with executable specifications. Many agile practitioners use the name Acceptance Test-Driven Development (ATDD) when requirements are automated into acceptance tests, which then drive the traditional test-driven development process [1]. To address the same needs, Dan North devised Behavior-Driven Development (BDD) where the business-facing tests are expressed as scenarios in a natural language that nonprogrammers can read [2]. In recent years, Gojko Adzic popularized an alternative description, "Specification by Example" [3]. In his book of the same title, he presented case studies of more than 50 teams successfully practicing this technique.

Many names reflect that there is a lot of innovation around executable specifications. Is there a difference between these three terms: test, scenario, and example? We hold them to be essentially the same thing because all three serve to illustrate user stories and are based on extensive collaboration. To be consistent, however, I had to choose one name. Scenario seems the best term: It is the easiest to understand for a nontechnical audience. In addition, I try to get away from the connotation linked to the word "test." It conveys the perception that it can be delayed during, or even after, the implementation. Using the word "scenario" amplifies the necessity to write actual scenarios during specifications and clarifies a lot of the confusion.

There are two scripting techniques with enough formalism to create a foundation on which you can automate validation. One has been popularized by Ward Cunningham and Rick Mugridge [4] and is referred to as the Framework for Integrated Test (FIT). It uses tables and analyzes scenarios, from left to right, within columns. The other is the Given-When-Then syntax, popularized by the Behavior-Driven Development (BDD) community [2]. This technique follows a top-to-bottom method of scripting an action.

Scripting Scenarios Using the FIT Tabular Format

Writing a scenario using a table is an effective and uncomplicated technique when obtaining a formal description from the stakeholders' perspective. This technique is central to FIT, an open-source tool for automating customer-facing tests. In this case, FIT enables you to write an acceptance test using a simple table, as shown in Figure 6.2.

Payment.Fixtures.BuyMonthlyPass		
Buyer	**Fare**	**Price?**
Student	Monthly Pass	$ 76
Senior	Monthly Pass	$ 98
Standard	Monthly Pass	$ 146

Figure 6.2 *A FIT table.*

These tables visually express, from left to right, and within columns, the preconditions and consequences that you find in a scenario. Because they are formalized using a well-defined tabular format, such scenarios are easy to maintain by people and are simple for tools to parse. Figure 6.3 helps to visualize this state transition.

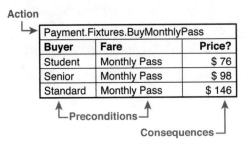

Figure 6.3 *A FIT table is a state transition.*

FIT enables the stakeholders, as well as the team, to illustrate each user story with a set of scenarios, formatted in tables and saved as HTML. Those scenarios are then connected to the software with programmer-written test fixtures and automatically checked for correctness. Every time the tests are run using FIT, the test runner automatically compares specifications to actual results and reports any errors by color-coding the table rows. Figure 6.4 shows how the test runner colors the tables green and red to highlight results (shown as light gray and dark gray in the printed book).

Payment.Fixtures.BuyMonthlyPass		
Buyer	**Fare**	**Price?**
Student	Monthly Pass	$ 76
Senior	Monthly Pass	$ 98
Standard	Monthly Pass	$ 146 Expected $ 134 Actual

Figure 6.4 *A FIT table is a test.*

Scripting Scenarios Using Given-When-Then Syntax

Around the same time FIT gained popularity, the BDD community started promoting the Given-When-Then syntax as a different technique for scripting scenarios. The following quote from David Chelimsky [5] summarizes BDD:

> "Behavior-Driven Development is about implementing an application by describing its behavior from the perspective of its stakeholders."

At the heart of this agile practice, the Given-When-Then syntax, using the Gherkin grammar [6], structures the description of the behavior expected by the stakeholders. It limits each scenario to only one transition. Because they are formalized using a well-known sequence, such scenarios, similar to FIT tabular format, are easy to maintain by people and simple for tools to parse.

The Given-When-Then syntax is expressed as follows:

```
Given one precondition
   And another precondition
   And yet another precondition
When an action occurs
Then a consequence
   And another consequence
```

Each clause is described here:

- **Given:** The necessary preconditions that put the system in a known state. These should define all and no more than the required context.

- **When:** The key action that creates a state transition. There should be only one action per scenario.

- **Then:** The consequences of the action. This is the observable outcome of the scenario.

- **And:** A placeholder that replaces "Given" or "Then" clauses when there are several of them.

Now imagine that you want to express the key scenarios for the following user story, "*As a student, I want to buy a monthly pass so that I go to school and get around.*" Here is an example written using the Given-When-Then syntax:

```
Given the buyer is a student
And the buyer selects a monthly pass
When the buyer pays
Then a sale occurs with an amount of 76 dollars
```

The Given-When-Then syntax is more verbose than a FIT tabular format. One benefit provided by FIT tabular format is that you can express several different values quickly only by adding new rows. A similar approach is offered with the Given-When-Then syntax through the use of a scenario outline, which acts as a template with placeholders. Placeholders must be contained within < > in the scenario steps.

As demonstrated in the following scenario outline, placeholders enable you to concisely express several different values with the use of an Example table.

```
Given the buyer is a <buyer_category>
And the buyer selects a monthly pass
When the buyer pays
Then a sale occurs with an amount of <price> dollars

Example:
    | buyer_category | price  |
    | Student        |  $76   |
    | Senior         |  $98   |
    | Standard       |  $146  |
```

Choosing Between FIT Tabular Format or Given-When-Then Syntax

Because there are two techniques for scripting scenarios, is one better than another? Unfortunately, both techniques have been evolving side by side for several years, and people tend to choose one technique over the other. The biggest misconception is to believe that one way is better than the other. The reality is these two techniques are equally effective. When you let go of such negative perceptions, you can use either technique to confirm your scenario with successful results. To demonstrate this, for the remainder of this chapter, I will script every scenario with both techniques, side by side.

Both techniques stimulate better thought processes because they raise the level of understanding closer to the problem's domain. Such emulation is valuable; it enables everyone to easily express the behavior of a domain. The strength of scripting scenarios with formal techniques is that it permits you to easily differentiate the key action from the preconditions and the consequences.

Formalizing a Ubiquitous Language

Particular attention should be given to naming concepts using domain vocabulary. A concept is a unit of meaning that expresses the behavior of the problem's domain. Each concept within a precondition, an action, or a consequence should have a unique name that follows the domain's terminology.

Most important, you must avoid duplicating the same concepts with different names. Do not assume you know the domain better than stakeholders do, even though they may disagree among themselves on the proper vocabulary. If in doubt, do not invent a new term; always use the language of the domain and seek agreement between stakeholders so that everyone uses a consistent vocabulary.

In addition to avoiding duplication, you must seek to limit the number of concepts by formalizing the language around the transition that occurs during the scenarios, whether it is scripted with the FIT tabular format or the Given-When-Then syntax. Transition is at the heart of what a scenario is. The action expresses the transition. A state is the result of the transition. States serve to represent the system both before and after the transition.

The use of states makes possible an evolution of the language, as shown in Figure 6.5. Preconditions states are the initial condition before action is taken, whereas consequence states expresses the resulting condition of the scenario. The action is the behavior performed by the scenario causing a transition to occur.

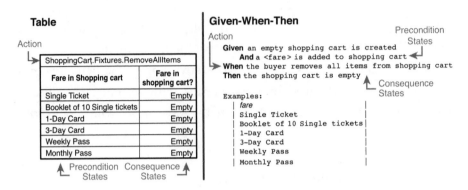

Figure 6.5 *Describing concepts using precondition and consequence states.*

The shift may seem subtle, but with scenarios that are expressed using states, you can formalize the language even more by differentiating the action from the preconditions and consequences.

The action represents the behavior causing a transition to occur during a scenario. Actions must always be verbs that are written in the present tense. The preconditions are states that already occurred in the past. They are also expressed as verbs, but as opposed to actions, they are not in the present tense.

This may seem trivial and even a bit redundant to express scenarios using the present tense, but this is the basis for formalizing a ubiquitous language. To illustrate, Figure 6.6 shows two scenarios demonstrating how an appropriate vocabulary creates a ubiquitous language. The vocabulary used to express a consequence can easily be reused as a precondition in a subsequent scenario.

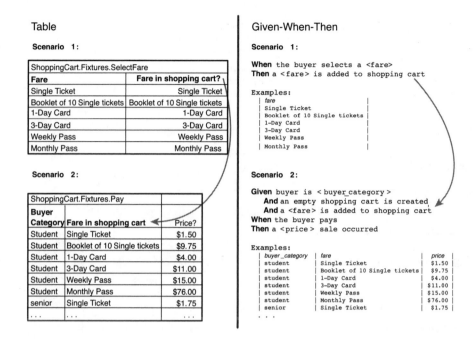

Figure 6.6 *Formalizing a ubiquitous language.*

Notice how "a <fare> is added to shopping cart" consistently connects the scenarios to create a ubiquitous language. By providing a common concept that both stakeholders and the team can read, communication is simplified.

Splitting Scenarios into Commands or Queries

If you want to create a more powerful ubiquitous language, you should recognize that only a small number of scenarios change the state of the system. Often, scenarios are queries that read only the state of the system and return a data-centric response. Only a small percentage of all the scenarios are a command that mutates the state.

By differentiating between command and query, you can be more precise with syntax and split the scenarios into two groups, as shown in Figure 6.7.

Table

Command:

ShoppingCart.Fixtures.aCommandAction				
Column 1	Column 2	. . .	column n-1?	Column n?
. . .	. . .	. . .	. . .	. . .
. . .	. . .	. . .	. . .	. . .
. . .	. . .	. . .	. . .	. . .

Query:

ShoppingCart.Fixtures.aQueryAction			
Column 1	Column 2	. . .	Column n
. . .	. . .	. . .	. . .
. . .	. . .	. . .	. . .
. . .	. . .	. . .	. . .

Given-When-Then

Command:

Given a set of *precondition states*
When a *command* occurs
Then a set of *consequence states*

Query:

Given a set of *precondition states*
When a *query* occurs
Then a *response* like
```
| Column 1 | Column 2 | . . .| Column n|
| . . .    | . . .    | . . .| . . .   |
| . . .    | . . .    | . . .| . . .   |
| . . .    | . . .    | . . .| . . .   |
```

Figure 6.7 *Differentiating between command and query.*

Often, when you use a query in a scenario, the answer is a list of items. Therefore, it is far simpler to express the response using a table. Figure 6.8 shows a scenario that demonstrates querying a list of items.

Table

ShoppingCart.Fixtures.ListOfStudentFares		
Id	Name	Price
001	Single Ticket	$1.50
002	Booklet of 10 Single tickets	$9.75
003	1-Day Card	$4.00
004	3-Day Card	$11.00
005	Weekly Pass	$15.00
006	Monthly Pass	$76.00

Given-When-Then

Given the buyer is a student
When the buyer requests the list of fares
Then *response* is
```
| Id  | Name                         | Price   |
| 001 | Single Ticket                | $1.50   |
| 002 | Booklet of 10 Single tickets | $9.75   |
| 003 | 1-Day Card                   | $4.00   |
| 004 | 3-Day Card                   | $11.00  |
| 005 | Weekly Pass                  | $15.00  |
| 006 | Monthly Pass                 | $76.00  |
```

Figure 6.8 *Querying a list of items.*

The first row is used to identify the contents of the columns, and each column contains the response value. This is different from a command scenario in which columns are a mix of preconditions and consequences.

As you will see in the next chapter, formalizing a ubiquitous language makes it easier to connect scenarios with code. It enables stakeholders to ensure their desirements are implemented as working software without any distortions.

Confirming Collaboratively in a Two-Step Process

Just like planning the tasks of a story occurs only when the team is ready to achieve it during the upcoming iteration, the team specifies the scenarios of a story at the last moment when all the ins and outs are known. This does not necessarily mean that you should wait until the beginning of a sprint to start confirming a user story with the key scenarios. However, it is important not to start too early because there's nothing more disheartening than taking the time to clarify the key scenarios and then realizing that the business value of a user story has changed and it needs to be reordered at the bottom of the backlog.

If the team is responsible for specifying at the last moment, how can it ensure that the scenarios are created in time? This requires a two-step process. Initially, you specify only the storyboard and the key scenarios. Subsequently, when a story is committed by the team for delivery, all the scenarios will be defined.

As shown in Figure 6.9, the first step occurs during backlog grooming when the storyboard and the key scenarios are defined collaboratively. The storyboard and the key scenarios identify and typically record representative behaviors that are required to fulfill a user story. These concrete examples are both the target for the development team and the success criteria for stakeholders to check whether the right software is being built.

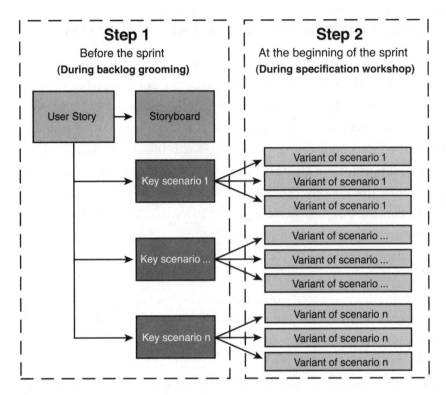

Figure 6.9 *Confirming collaboratively using a two-step process.*

Grooming is used to obtain a healthy backlog; that is to say, a properly ordered list of desirements sufficiently specified with concrete examples so that the team can plan and deliver them as promised in a sprint. The outputs produced during grooming are just enough concrete examples for the team to properly assess efforts and size a user story.

The second step, also shown in Figure 6.9, is when a story has been planned by the team for delivery. As soon as possible, when the iteration starts, the development team must complete each key scenario by identifying the different variations. As said by Gojko Adzic [7], a successful team refines the concrete examples and adds all the variants.

> "Successful teams don't use raw examples, they refine the specification from them. They extract the essence from the key examples and turn them into a clear and unambiguous definition of what makes the implementation done, without any extraneous detail."

As shown in Figure 6.10, specifying the scenarios is accomplished the first day of the sprint, prior to the sprint planning, by scheduling a Specification Workshop to handle this important step.

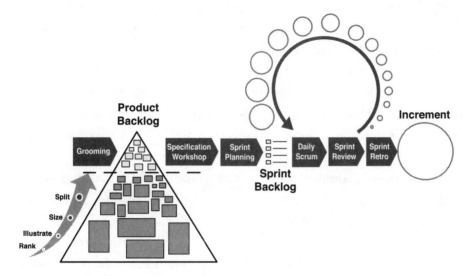

Figure 6.10 *Specifying the scenarios.*

You should conduct a workshop—not only with all team members, but also with stakeholders such as domain experts, end users, or salesmen. Only stakeholders who add value to the workshop are invited. The major benefit of planning a workshop is that it makes effective use of the stakeholders' time. Because they have their own daily jobs that already monopolize them, bottlenecks often occur. As said by Gojko Adzic [8], the workshop is a good opportunity to get their attention early in the sprint.

> "The goal of the workshop is to build a shared understanding of the problem and the solution and to make sure that all the functional gaps are identified early, not later in the iteration, when business people might not be readily available."

For a specification workshop to function properly, it must be preplanned by the product owner. Stakeholders need to be invited ahead of time for this because if they do not attend, it will be difficult to conduct the meeting. Try to limit the meetings to no more than two hours because after that much time people tend to be less productive.

The purpose of the meeting is to review as many user stories as possible. Each user story will be reviewed, one at a time for priority. While reviewing each user story, all team members get the opportunity to refamiliarize themselves with the storyboard.

A good practice, during the specification workshop, is to name an analyst for each user story. The analyst is always a member of the development team. This responsibility should never be given to a stakeholder because it is time-consuming, and this increases the risk that the specification will not be completed in a timely manner. It is important to note that the analyst's competency is related to the specifications and not to how the software will be implemented. After the meeting, all analysts must finalize the scenarios for their user story.

A good candidate for an analyst is a team member with a strong background as a business analyst. Business analysts usually have the skills for this type of responsibility. Being an analyst for the user story does not mean that you work alone. To refine a scenario, collaboration with stakeholders and team members is mandatory.

Every user story has one storyboard and several key scenarios that illustrate the story. The members of the meeting determine whether the storyboard is complete. During that time, stakeholders have the opportunity to give their feedback. A question that may arise in the process is whether key scenarios are missing. If this is the case, the team members can add those elements into the story. The team then moves on to another story. Each of these steps is repeated for every user story.

The discussion period should be quick, so rather than taking notes and wasting time, record with a voice recorder what is said so that all the information about the scenarios is registered. Because of time constraints, the refinement and polishing of the scenarios in a story are rarely completed during the workshop. However, the functional gaps are always discussed. A lot of detailed work must be completed by the analysts in the days following the meeting.

Though it is rare that all the user stories are covered in depth during this two-hour period, the ones that are planned for implementation in the upcoming sprint should have been discussed. An organized team should be disciplined enough to get through all these stories during the meeting. Not covering all user stories happens only if the meeting has been badly managed by the Scrum master and the product owner.

What Is the New Role of Business Analysts?

In the traditional requirements-gathering process, a business analyst is an expert hired to translate information between stakeholders and the team. Under this scheme, there is the belief that the two groups cannot understand each other.

Within an agile framework, business analysts are no longer the conveyor of information but facilitators that organize the transfer of knowledge and chase open issues. The role of business analysts is now more focused and can be summarized as ensuring that all the scenarios illustrating a story are refined and completed in time for the development team.

Removing Technical Considerations from Scenarios

After the decision on how the user interface should behave is encapsulated in the storyboard, the stakeholders should feel comfortable describing what the key scenarios are supposed to do. As said previously, early in the sprint, the analysts simplify the scenarios by concisely describing the stakeholders' intentions.

There are different levels of abstraction when expressing scenarios, as shown in Figure 6.11. This varies in terms of the technical considerations involved. Because designing the technical solution is not the purpose of the specification, you should focus only on writing scenarios that relate to the business rules. This does not mean you should not focus on the user experience; storyboards are used for that.

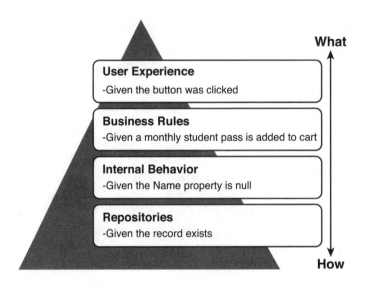

Figure 6.11 *Scenarios work at many levels.*

Avoid Adding Scenarios Related to Technical Issues

During the sprint, and as early as possible, all the business-oriented scenarios will be produced. At this point, it can be tempting to add scenarios related to technical issues. The analysts must resist this temptation.

The development of the scenarios is a collaborative and iterative work. During this process, the team must remember that scenarios are used to specify the stakeholders' desirements and not to design the solution. As part of an iterative process in which the work is spread over a few weeks, there is a thin line between specification and implementation. You cross the line typically when you start thinking about the solution in terms of technical issues. For example, answering questions such as how to save and retrieve data is not appropriate at this stage.

Whenever possible, avoid scripting scenarios that describe internal behaviors or technical issues. It is important that the scenarios focus on the business rules and stay at this level of abstraction. This ensures stakeholders and the whole team understand the domain functionalities the same way. A good approach when transforming scenarios expressed in technical terms, is the 5 Whys analysis method. Asking "Why?" five times, successively, helps the team understand the true root cause of the scenario and easily reformulate it at the business domain level. Removing the technical considerations simplifies the transformation of the scenarios into acceptance tests, as explained in the following chapter.

Keep in mind that during the remainder of the sprint, the analysts finalize the scenarios ensuring each one is autonomous and free of technical considerations. Hopefully, by the end of the sprint, not only each scenario is complete, but also each story is ready to be delivered.

Evolving Scenarios from Sprint to Sprint

From sprint to sprint, the team builds the software from small and potentially disjointed stories. The challenges faced after several sprints are how to avoid duplication, merge conflicts, and get a coherent view of all the behaviors. Behaviors related to the user experience are not problematic because they are easily accessible through the software. As a result, you do not need to track the storyboards. However, when taking into consideration the business rules, the software is not sufficient in terms of grasping all the subtleties of the behavior. As a result, the team needs to keep track of all the scenarios. Therefore, the scenarios are a permanent specification that not only must be accessible during the entire life of the software but should also be organized and easily searchable.

Organizing Scenarios by Feature

As much as they are useful from the point of view of the team delivering the sprint, desirements expressed as stories are not the best technique for permanently organizing the scenarios. Stories are used to subdivide, prioritize, and plan the incremental development of the software. They are useful for tracking work, and it is important to safeguard this information. However, a higher level of abstraction, more useful from the stakeholders' perspective, is necessary.

As shown in Figure 6.12, features provide this level of abstraction. A feature is a piece of high-level functionality that delivers value to one or more stakeholders. As presented in the previous chapter, features are unlikely to change over time. Features are used to split desirements along the process lines when story mapping. A feature is a business activity in the process lines that separates into several stories. Features integrate stories and scenarios in a coherent fashion from sprint to sprint because they are a permanent unit of classification that stakeholders can easily understand.

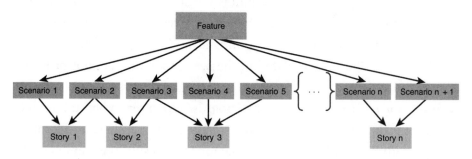

Figure 6.12 *Organizing the scenarios by feature.*

Linking scenarios to features helps to structure a hierarchy, thereby simplifying the query process. As shown in Figure 6.13, the important link that absolutely needs to be established is the one between the scenario and the feature. It should be unique. A scenario should validate only one feature.

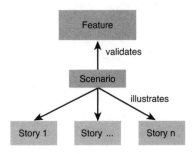

Figure 6.13 *A scenario validates only one feature.*

Documenting Scenarios by Feature

With the appropriate software tools, you can store the specification in a database and tag each scenario with its feature. On-the-fly, when required, these computer-based tools make it possible for everyone to easily generate the overall specifications documentation. Because this documentation is always up to date, it is a reliable and authoritative source of information on software functionality. To provide a glimpse of what the documentation might look like, Figure 6.14 shows a sample for the feature "Shopping Cart" in the "MTA Self-Serve Smartcard Ticketing Kiosk."

Feature: Shopping Cart

| Scenario |

```
Given the buyer is a student
When the buyer requests the list of fares
Then response is
   | Id  | Name                      | Price   |
   | 001 | Single Ticket             | $1.50   |
   | 002 | Booklet of 10 Single tickets| $9.75 |
   | 003 | 1-Day Card                | $4.00   |
   | 004 | 3-Day Card                | $11.00  |
   | 005 | Weekly Pass               | $15.00  |
   | 006 | Monthly Pass              | $76.00  |
```

Story : As a student, I want to buy a transit fare so that I can go to school and get around

| Scenario |

```
When the buyer selects a <fare>
Then a <fare> is added to shopping cart

Examples:
   | fare                          |
   | Single Ticket                 |
   | Booklet of 10 Single tickets  |
   | 1-Day Card                    |
   | 3-Day Card                    |
   | Weekly Pass                   |
   | Monthly Pass                  |
```

Story : As a student, I want to buy a transit fare so that I can go to school and get around

| Scenario |

```
Given the buyer is <buyer_category>
   And an empty shopping cart is created
   And a <fare> is added to shopping cart
When the buyer pays
Then a <price> sale occurred

Examples:
   | buyer_category | fare                       | price   |
   | student        | Single Ticket              | $1.50   |
   | student        | Booklet of 10 Single tickets| $9.75  |
   | student        | 1-Day Card                 | $4.00   |
   | student        | 3-Day Card                 | $11.00  |
   | student        | Weekly Pass                | $15.00  |
   | student        | Monthly Pass               | $76.00  |
```

Story: As a student, I want to buy a transit fare so that I can go to school and get around

Figure 6.14 *Generating the specification with computer-based tools.*

Avoiding Duplication and Merging Conflicts

When an analyst inherits the scenarios produced during the specification workshop, the first thing to do is to review all scenarios within the feature to which the story belongs. Often, there will be scenarios that closely resemble the new scenario. In this case, it is simply a question of refactoring the scenarios to avoid duplicates. However, sometimes one new scenario will be in conflict with one or more existing scenarios. In this case, the analyst must identify not only the scenario, but also the stories that are in conflict. Then the analyst should revive the conversation with the product owner who decides the best course of action.

Summary

In this chapter, you learned to confirm user stories with scenarios. Scenarios complement a user story and its storyboard by scripting concrete exercises written in everyday language. Scenarios formalize the description of the behavior expected by the stakeholders using a cause-and-effect transition. A scenario contains precondition states, an action, and consequence states. We have demonstrated how to formalize scenarios using a FIT tabular format and the Given-When-Then syntax.

This chapter explained how both scripting techniques formalize a ubiquitous language only if you limit the number of concepts, avoid duplicating the same concepts with different names, and differentiate between commands and queries. A concept is a unit of meaning that expresses the behavior of the problem's domain. Using domain vocabulary, concepts gives a unique name to states and actions that make up a scenario.

You have learned that confirming stories is a two-step process. Initially, you start by specifying only the storyboard and the key scenarios. Subsequently, when a story is planned by the team for delivery, you finalize all the scenarios during a specification workshop.

You learned that a specification workshop brings together, at the beginning of the sprint, the team and stakeholders to create a shared understanding of all the scenarios that are to be delivered during the sprint. The workshop makes effective use of the stakeholders' precious time. Refinement and polishing of the scenarios will be completed by the analysts during the sprint.

Finally, this chapter explained that to avoid duplication, merge conflicts, and get a coherent view of all the behaviors from sprint to sprint, the requirements specification should be organized by feature. A feature is a piece of high-level functionality that delivers value to one or more stakeholders. A feature is a business activity that separates into several stories. Because they are a permanent unit of classification that stakeholders can easily understand, features integrate stories and scenarios in a coherent fashion.

In the next chapter, you will discover how scenarios are the foundation upon which you can automate confirmation and how these scenarios are both, at the same time, a confirmation of success criteria and a future regression test.

References

[1]   Acceptance Test-Driven Development, http://en.wikipedia.org/wiki/Test-driven_development

[2]   North, Dan (2006). "Introducing BDD." http://dannorth.net/introducing-bdd/

[3]   Adzic, Gojko (2011). *Specification by Example: How Successful Teams Deliver the Right Software*. Greenwich, CT: Manning Publications.

[4]   Mugridge, Rick, Ward Cunningham (2005). *Fit for Developing Software: Framework for Integrated Tests*. Upper Saddle River, NJ: Prentice Hall.

[5]   Chelimsky, David (2010). *The RSpec Book: Behaviour Driven Development with Rspec, Cucumber, and Friends*. Raleigh, NC: Pragmatic Bookshelf.

[6]   Hellesoy, Aslak (2010). "Gherkin." https://github.com/aslakhellesoy/cucumber/wiki/gherkin

[7]   Adzic, Gojko (2009). *Bridging the Communication Gap: Specification by Example and Agile Acceptance Testing*. London, UK: Neuri Limited.

Chapter 7

Automating Confirmation with Acceptance Tests

The previous chapter explained that scenarios assist in monitoring the conversation and confirming expectations. At this point, you understand that scenarios express the success criteria of what is delivered during the sprint. This chapter aims to go further by automating confirmation. You can confirm with an acceptance test that the success criteria are met. This chapter addresses the following quality assurance challenges. How do you confirm repeatedly and on a recurring basis that the software always meets the evolving specifications? This is even more problematic to the extent that it's often extremely difficult to figure out how a change in one part of the software can echo in other parts that have been developed during previous sprints. In other words, how do you make sure when adding a new user story that the preceding stories are still valid?

Automating confirmation is the main theme of this chapter, which is done by turning scenarios into acceptance tests. This chapter explains how to make the scenarios "executable" by a computer. In doing so, you learn that this requires a three-stage process that has many similarities with the red-green-refactor cycle popularized by Test-Driven Development practices. The core of this chapter presents this three-stage process. This chapter concludes by explaining that "executable" scenarios require a test environment that is different from the continuous integration environment. This testing environment ensures that you easily gather tests results and enhance executable specifications with valuable feedback.

Evolving Scenarios into Acceptance Tests

Given that the goal is to build the right software, it makes perfect sense, periodically and on a recurring basis, to confirm that all the scenarios are implemented correctly by the evolving software. However, how do you do this without taking up too much of the team's precious time? The manual execution of these confirmations would jeopardize the sprint, slow down feedback, and introduce unnecessary delays. Though common sense might tell us to automate these confirmations with acceptance tests, acceptance tests should not become a new specification.

You must turn scenarios into acceptance tests with minimal changes. An acceptance test is only a copy of a scenario in a format suitable for execution on a computer. An acceptance test must look like the original scenario, even if there are constraints related with the programming language. The idea is to avoid distortions that create cognitive dissonance (discomfort caused by holding conflicting beliefs or ideas simultaneously). As we all know, when there is more than one version of the truth, there are synchronization issues.

As shown in Figure 7.1, an acceptance test is the act of executing a scenario to confirm the story has been implemented as specified.

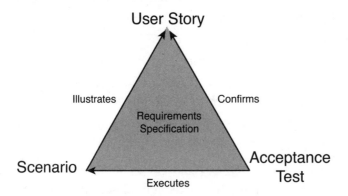

Figure 7.1 *The acceptance test is a copy of a scenario in a format suitable for execution on a computer.*

An acceptance test is a scenario executed by a computer to confirm that the team is building the right software and is satisfying stakeholders' desirements. We acknowledge that this definition of a test is conceptually different from traditional test automation. The intent is not to verify whether the team is building the software correctly. First and foremost, we want to confirm requirements have been met. These "executable" scenarios are not a quality assurance tool. They are used to prevent defects, not to discover them. They act as functional regression tests to verify there are no incongruities with the specifications. In this regard, these "executable" scenarios do not replace the need to include quality assurance practices, such as exploratory or unit testing.

Unlike stories and scenarios, which are stored as work items in a specification repository, acceptance tests are programming code and as such are stored in version control. Because automating confirmation deals with programming, you must rely on a proven development cycle. Furthermore, because you prioritize making code correctly before making it well, the development cycle must help in this manner. Now see in more detail what this means.

At the beginning of the sprint, during a specifications workshop, the team creates scenarios and, with the help of stakeholders, makes certain assumptions about the desirable outcome of a user story. Later, during the sprint, the programmer reads the scenarios and foresees a solution. He thinks about the big picture using the scenario as a guideline and breaks it up into small accessible problems (basic problem solving). At that point, the foreseen behavior already implies a set of different assumptions, technical for the most part.

The programmer dives right in and starts building a solution to tackle one of these small problems. Obviously, the programmer's assumptions affect the behavior of the small solution in such a way that is difficult to forecast. Then, he tests her small solution to make sure it works and provokes more thought on how it fits into the big picture. Unfortunately, unit tests do not help in this matter. Unit tests always pass because they test against the programmer's assumptions. When happy with the result, the programmer tackles the next small problem. He then constantly reassesses the big picture, identify emerging issues and adding new assumptions.

After the scenario is implemented by the programmer, the tester gets involved to create acceptance tests. He reads the scenarios, assesses the solution produced by the programmer, and makes a third set of assumptions. Finally, all these assumptions are revised at the end of the sprint during the sprint review. Unfortunately for the team, assumptions are not synced up until later in the process. This produces imperfect code that rarely solves accurately the stakeholders' problems.

The development cycle must help synchronize the development team's assumptions early. The team needs faster feedback loops for discovering whether an implementation is correct for the scenario's assumptions.

It goes without saying that the widespread approach of creating tests using record-and-playback tools is inappropriate. These tools record mouse movements and mouse clicks and replay the sequence of user actions as if they were executed directly by the user. They also check results, such as whether expected texts appear on the screen. Their main advantage, which is to enable testers to author tests without having to learn how to craft code, is also their main weakness. Authoring is possible only with a completely finished implementation. It is effective for discovering defects, not for preventing them. It is of no help when the need is to validate assumptions during implementation.

Everything leads you to rely on a test-first approach. The red-green-refactor cycle, popularized by the Test-Driven Development practices, is well suited for this goal. As such, it is going to drive how you turn a scenario into an acceptance test.

From day one, you start by translating the scenario into an acceptance test. Next, use this acceptance test for monitoring assumptions, giving developers useful and quick feedback during implementation, and making sure they are on the right path. Then, when an assumption about the desirable outcome happens to be wrong, the team can use the test results to understand why the implementation is doing what it's doing.

Acceptance tests represent assumptions stakeholders made during the specification. If acceptance tests are successful, they are proof that the assumptions still hold true in the implementation. As the team adds new stories or refactors the existing code, the old acceptance tests automatically verify the past assumptions.

Automating Scenarios Using the Red-Green-Refactor Cycle

The red-green-refactor cycle is the core of Test-Driven Development (TDD). It is a widely recognized programming practice popularized by Kent Beck [1] that promotes the notion of writing tests first when programming a piece of code. TDD relies on the repetition of a short development cycle divided into three stages: the red, the green, and the refactor stage.

1. **Red:** Start by translating into a test the assumptions about the externally visible behavior of the piece of code that will be implemented. Then, make it fail (calibrate the failed test). Because there is only an interface contract with no implementation, it is foreseeable that the test will fail. This is proof that you seek. You expect that when there is a fault, the test will be unsuccessful. This is what you calibrate first.

2. **Green:** Continue by writing the simplest implementation to make the test pass. (Calibrate the passing test.) Aim to complete the calibration of the test, with minimal risk, by making it successful using simple implementation.

3. **Refactor:** Tooled with a calibrated test that acts as a safety net, you can now reorganize the simplest implementation to eliminate duplication and allow patterns to emerge using experiments. Make small improvements one at a time, always complying with the initial assumptions and making sure that the test is successful after each little improvement.

TDD works because it forces programmers to define, at a level of precision not generally covered by the specification, what they expect the unit to do. TDD requires programmers to articulate their assumptions using a test case. Programmers must foresee how the functionality will be used by the test case. TDD places constraints on programmers; it requires that they define the interface before deciding on the implementation. TDD tends to lead to better designs. It makes code inherently reusable because programmers must use it in both tests and production circumstances.

TDD is a practice designed to help with unit testing. Now see how it can help automate confirmation with acceptance tests.

As shown in Figure 7.2, turning scenarios into acceptance tests is a three-stage process with strong similarities to the red-green-refactor cycle.

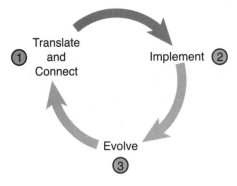

Figure 7.2 *Turning scenarios into acceptance tests using a three-stage process.*

Now look at each stage in a little more detail:

1. **Translate and connect (Red):** While keeping the original intent and without distorting the assumptions of the scenario, begin by translating the scenario into an acceptance test. Connect the newly created acceptance test to the programming interface of the new piece of code. When the acceptance test is written, run it and watch the new test fail: The test bar should turn red. This ends the first step of the calibration.

2. **Implement (Green):** Complete the second step of calibration by making the test successful. Produce the simplest code to make the failing test pass. After this simple implementation is done, run the test and watch it pass: The test bar turns green.

3. **Evolve (Refactor):** Guided by the newly calibrated test, remove the technical debt induced by the simple implementation. Rearrange the inner workings of the test by making small changes one step at a time. Rely on the calibrated test by always ensuring that the acceptance test passes after each little refactoring.

As shown in Figure 7.3, this red-green-refactor cycle occurs during the sprint repeatedly and on a regular basis. Actually, this is how a software increment is built by the development team. The team translates the scenario into an acceptance test, connects it with the software increment, implements the software increment, and evolves it. This cycle is repeated for each scenario and for each user story.

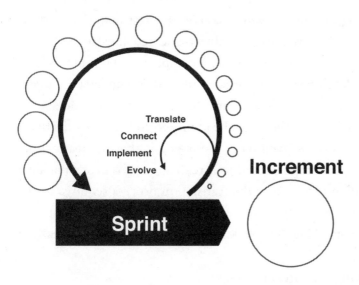

Figure 7.3 *Turning scenarios into acceptance tests is how an increment is built.*

The next section explains in more detail how to perform each stage of this cycle.

Translating the Scenario into an Acceptance Test

During the "red" stage, the tester develops an acceptance test by following a specific sequence of steps that impose constraints. These constraints exist to ensure that the many technical assumptions that are selected during the design do not cause the implementation to diverge from the original intent of the scenario. The most important constraint to consider here is how to force a design on the interface before the implementation of the code. Before reaching this milestone, however, there are prerequisites. You must, as a first step, translate the scenario into an acceptance test.

The challenge during translation is to ensure that the newly created test demonstrates the same expected behavior as the scenario. Unlike storyboards, where the behavior is sketched with pictures, there is no visual aid for programming scenarios. The acceptance test comes down to pure programming.

Often, the pursuit of efficiency can force the testers to use the same general-purpose programming language to write the acceptance test as they use to program the software. Today, the vast majority of these programming languages are based on object-oriented constructs. Unfortunately, these programming languages are complex, and it is almost certain that only the developers have the skills to read and understand them.

If the development team members are the only ones who understand the result of the translation, they lose the ability to collaborate effectively with stakeholders. What is even more damaging is that the team could easily align on false assumptions without realizing it. To protect against this risk, the solution is to ensure the translation process requires no assumptions. This is achievable with the aid of a domain-specific language (DSL) that is tailor-made for this task and easy to master by the team.

Transposing Using an Internal DSL

Martin Fowler defines a DSL as a computer programming language of limited vocabulary that is focused on a particular domain [2]. The DSL that the team wants to build should provide minimal capabilities needed to translate a scenario into a test executable by a computer. It needs to be a front end that connects into the source code with the same syntax as the one used to express the scenarios.

To reuse the team's skills and reduce accidental complexity induced by an external DSL, the simplest solution is to embed an internal DSL within the programming language already in use by the team. An internal DSL is a DSL represented within the syntax of a general-purpose language. By using only a subset of the host language's features, the result should have the feel of a custom language.

As a general rule, translating scenarios into acceptance tests should require no technical assumptions. One way of doing that is to integrate with existing tooling through the help of a BDD automation framework. There are BDD automation frameworks for each major programming platform. The best known are Cucumber for Ruby [3], JBehave for Java [4], and SpecFlow for Microsoft .NET [5]. Besides the fact that the team can leverage its programming and environmental capabilities, one of the main advantages of building an internal DSL with a BDD automation framework is the team does not need to provide a mechanism to drive the application under test, execute the acceptance tests, and report results. Furthermore, when developing the syntax of the internal DSL, the team can take advantage of the common conventions in a developer's regular life. For example, if the team uses Java or C#, then you can use "//" for your comments and "{" and "}" for any hierarchical structures.

Now see how to set up an internal DSL with well-known, general-purpose programming languages. For the benefit of the demonstration, here is the scenario you use:

```
Given an empty shopping cart is created
    And a monthly student pass is added to shopping cart
When the buyer checks out the shopping cart
Then a 76 dollar sale occurs
```

Each internal DSL is unique and the solution must fit the context. For the case of translating scenarios into acceptance tests, there are two proven and recognized approaches to designing an internal DSL: pattern matching and fluent interface.

If the team uses a dynamic language, such as Ruby, the simplest way to create an internal DSL is to use the pattern-matching capabilities already included in the host programming language. Here is a first demonstration that translates the Given-When-Then scenario inside the Ruby host programming language. Notice how regular expressions are used to define method parameters.

```
Given /^an empty shopping cart is created $/ do
   ...
End
Given /^ a (.*) is added to shopping cart $/ do |pass|
   ...
End
When /^the buyer checks out the shopping cart $/ do
   ...
End
Then /^a ([0-9]*) dollar sale occurs $/ do |amount|
   ...
End
```

If the team uses a strongly typed language, such as Java or C#, and it wants to build an internal DSL using the "pattern matching" paradigm, it must rely on annotations. Annotations, which are called *custom attributes* on the .Net platform, enable developers to add metadata to the host code programming elements. Here is a second demonstration that translates the Given-When-Then scenario within the Java host programming language using pattern matching and annotations:

```
@Given ("^an empty shopping cart is created $")
 public void GivenAnEmptyShoppingCartIsCreated ()
 {
   ...
 }
@Given ("^a (.*)is added to shopping cart $")
 public void GivenA_IsAddedToShoppingCart (string pass)
 {
   ...
 }
@When ("^the buyer checks out the shopping cart$")
 public void WhenTheBuyerChecksOutTheShoppingCart()
 {
   ...
 }
@Then ("^a ([0-9]*) dollar sale occurs$")
 public void ThenA_DollarSaleOccurs (money amount)
 {
   ...
 }
```

One challenge with pattern matching is knowing how to map an English sentence via regular expressions. The internal DSL must be tightly controlled so that managing the mapping doesn't get out of hand. At any time, if you change a sentence, you have to find the method that directly relates to that sentence and fix the regular expression matching. This is why I prefer implementing an internal DSL with the help of a fluent interface.

A fluent interface relies upon method chaining. It uses a sequence of method calls where each call acts upon the result of the previous calls. It is a style of manipulation that resembles the process of putting together whole sentences. Here is a third demonstration that translates the Given-When-Then scenario using a fluent interface within the C# host programming language.

```
new Scenario("Feature: Shopping Cart")
    .Given(AnEmptyShoppingCartIsCreated )
    .Given(APassIsAddedToShoppingCart, pass: "student monthly
            pass" )
    .When(TheBuyerChecksOutTheShoppingCart)
    .Then(ANumberDollarSaleOccurs, number: 76)
    .Execute();
```

In addition to eliminating regular expressions, and the problems this generates, the major benefit of a fluent interface is that the translation is explicit. The differences between the acceptance test and the original scenario are almost unnoticeable from the developers' point of view. Even if the Given-When-Then scenario is now embedded within a complex programming language, the team can easily verify that it complies with the original intent.

Creating a Test

When creating an acceptance test, never forget that the team's goal is to achieve test execution with minimal effort. We have already described why the team should opt to build an internal DSL using a BDD automation framework. Now, we'll explain how the team should take advantage of this automation framework.

The BDD automation framework provides a mechanism that hooks into the application under test, executes the tests, and reports results. Figure 7.4 shows how testers can embed a scenario inside the SpecFlow [5] automation framework by using the C# host programming language that comes with the Microsoft .Net platform. The Binding annotation (marker #1) creates a link to the SpecFlow automation framework. Furthermore, the Given-When-Then annotation (marker #2) enables the team to easily instantiate the scenarios and execute them within the testing environment.

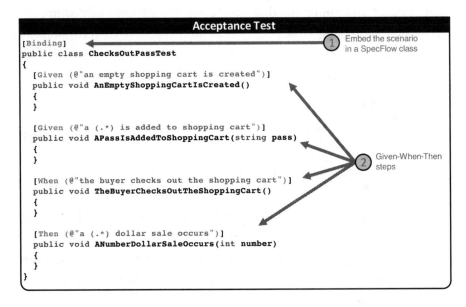

Figure 7.4 *Coding the internal DSL inside the SpecFlow automation framework.*

Coding the DSL into the Newly Created Test

Transposing the Given-When-Then steps using an internal DSL is what can convince the team that the newly created acceptance test confirms the same behavior as the scenario, and without any false assumptions.

Figure 7.5 shows a second example of an internal DSL. This time the testers code the internal DSL using a fluent interface as defined by the StoryQ [6] automation framework. You can translate the Given-When-Then steps by embedding the scenario (marker #1) into the newly created acceptance test and by creating a private method for each step (marker #2).

```
                          Acceptance Test
[TestClass]
public class ChecksOutPassTest
{
  [TestMethod]
  public void ChecksOutPassScenario()
  {
    new Story("Transit Fare")
        .InOrderTo("go to school and get around")
        .AsA("student")
        .IWantTo("buy a transit fare")
        .WithScenario("Checkout pass")          ◄──────  ①  Scenario express using a DSL
          .Given(AnEmptyShoppingCartIsCreated)
            .And(APassIsAddedToShoppingCart, pass: "student monthly pass")
          .When(TheBuyerChecksOutTheShoppingCart)
          .Then(ANumberDollarSaleOccurs, number: 76)
          .ExecuteWithReport(MethodBase.GetCurrentMethod());
  }

  void AnEmptyShoppingCartIsCreated ()
  {
  }
  void APassIsAddedToShoppingCart (string pass)      ②  Given-When-Then steps
  {
  }
  void TheBuyerChecksOutTheShoppingCart()
  {
  }
  void ANumberDollarSaleOccurs(int number)
  {
  }
}
```

Figure 7.5 *Coding the internal DSL inside the StoryQ automation framework.*

This completes what must be done to translate the scenario into an acceptance test. However, if the tester runs this test, it will not fail. Obtaining a failing test is the expected behavior during the "red" stage. This requires the tester to go one step further than translating. To obtain a failing assertion, the tester must design the programming interface and connect the newly created test with it.

Connecting the Newly Created Test with the Interface

Unlike translation, connecting the test with the software is much more challenging. The task is further complicated because the software's internal implementation does not exist. Fortunately, the software's externally visible behavior is more important than its internal structure. When connecting the newly created test, the tester focuses first on defining the outside-facing programming interface and only after that does the programmer go on evolving the internal implementation. When connecting, the work is summed by identifying the abstractions representing what needs to be as well as the programming interface that governs them.

This programming interface can take many forms. For example, if the team builds a console application, the tester can connect the test by running a command line. Similarly, if the team builds a web application, the tester can rely on the HTTP request. Finally, in a more complex case, the tester can decide to bypass the user interface and connect the test directly to the application's controller. In all cases, the real challenge is to properly design the programming interface.

The natural candidates for this type of design are the testers because they are the ones responsible for creating a failing acceptance test. They have the expertise to abstract what is required by the scenario and create a visible interface to satisfy it. However, you must not forget that this design duty is a specification responsibility. The goal is not to program a complete implementation but instead to define the contract between the acceptance test and the software. As all experienced developers might say, it is a job that requires more skill in architecture than in programming. That is why when the work is challenging, testers must collaborate with architects to identify the optimal solution.

Architecting the Programming Interface

Sometimes, the easiest way to test a scenario is to bypass the user interface completely. Unfortunately, in the absence of a thoughtful architecture, the user interface is tightly coupled with the rest of the application. This requires the introduction of software architecture to decouple the business logic from the user interface.

One option is to separate the application into three independent modules: the view, the controller, and the model. The view is where the user interface is displayed. The controller is where the behaviors to connect with the rest of the application are located. The model is the data that needs to be shared between the view and the controller. This design pattern, which not surprisingly is called Model-View-Controller, is well known and has been widely adopted since the early days of computing.

The classic Model-View-Controller pattern is rarely used today in its original form; though, it has given rise to a number of variations adapted to newer development platforms. The Model-View-Presenter (MVP) is well suited when programming GUI applications, whereas the Model-View-Controller (MVC) with URL routing is the de facto standard for web applications. Do not overlook the Model-View-ViewModel (MVVM), which is becoming increasingly popular with the rise of platforms using markup language for UI display.

By applying an architecture based on Model-View-Controller, testers can easily bypass the user interface and ensure that the application's controller provides a programming interface for testing scenarios.

Exercising the Interface

Because the aim of each scenario is to execute code within the software, it is natural that the internal DSL connects to the software. Only behaviors related to the acceptance test lie in the DSL. As shown in Figure 7.6, whenever possible, the behavior in the internal DSL should be lightweight. As the three markers, #1, #2, and #3, demonstrate, the DSL is only a front end built specifically for exercising the software.

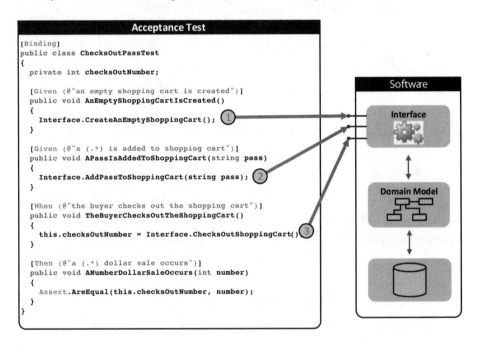

Figure 7.6 *Connecting the steps with the interface.*

Because there is almost a direct link to the programming interface, it is natural that the interface uses the same names for concepts as in scenarios. There is no benefit in creating accidental complexity by using a different naming scheme for the same concepts. How testers architect the programming interface can significantly reduce the complexity required to connect the scenarios with source code. At this point, what is important to understand is that the DSL connects with the software; the architectural considerations are beyond the scope of this book.

Connecting Acceptance Tests to the Domain Model

In a layered architecture, the programming interface is a thin layer at the top that serves as a gateway to the domain model. This visible interface does not contain business logic but coordinates tasks for the users and delegates to work on the domain model in the next layer down. The only states that the programming interface manages relate to the user interactions.

The term *domain model* can mean different things to different people, depending on their programming background. For some, it is a data-centric conceptual model that describes various entities included in the problem domain. For others, and this book is adopting this terminology, a domain model is a web of interconnected objects that encapsulates the core behaviors needed to solve problems in a domain. Martin Fowler, in his book *Patterns of Enterprise Application Architecture*, defined the domain model as the space where the team captures the core behavior of a software system [7].

Implementing a programming interface isn't mandatory; it is only there if it adds value. So, if it simplifies programming, it is okay to connect an acceptance test directly to the domain model.

Chaining Context Between the Steps of the Scenario

While programming the acceptance test, often testers need to share context between each of the steps in the scenario. Figure 7.7 demonstrates one of the great benefits of encapsulating the DSL inside a class. The class provides a private context for sharing information between the steps. Marker #1 shows how an internal context variable is initialized during the "When" step, whereas marker #2 shows how the same internal context variable is used later during the "Then" step.

Acceptance Test

```
[Binding]
public class ChecksOutPassTest
{
  private int checksOutNumber;

  [Given (@"an empty shopping cart is created")]
  public void AnEmptyShoppingCartIsCreated()
  {
    Interface.CreateAnEmptyShoppingCart();
  }

  [Given (@"a (.*) is added to shopping cart")]
  public void APassIsAddedToShoppingCart(string pass)
  {
    Interface.AddPassToShoppingCart(string pass);
  }

  [When (@"the buyer checks out the shopping cart")]
  public void TheBuyerChecksOutTheShoppingCart()
  {
    this.checksOutNumber = Interface.ChecksOutShoppingCart();
  }

  [Then (@"a (.*) dollar sale occurs")]
  public void ANumberDollarSaleOccurs(int number)
  {
    Assert.AreEqual(this.checksOutNumber, number);
  }
}
```

Figure 7.7 *Chaining context between the steps.*

Making the Test Fail

During the "red" stage, it is too easy to think that the only goal is to create a test. There is much more to this. Testers start with a test that fails to calibrate it. Because there is no behavior that has been implemented behind the programming interface, it is foreseeable that the test will fail. This is the proof that testers seek. They expect that the test will be unsuccessful when there is a fault. This is what testers calibrate first.

Implementing the Interface

As soon as a programmer starts programming the behavior behind the interface, you enter the "green" stage. During the "green" stage, the programmer wants to complete the calibration of the failed test by making it successful. The aim is to make the test pass by coding the simplest thing that works. This implementation helps to demonstrate that the test is well calibrated.

Even if you strive for simplicity, in most cases, this behavior is complex and requires mastering the business logic as well as mastering the technical issues. Completing a scenario can easily require several hours of programming. The programmer has no other choice but to rely on a divide and conquer approach. Inevitably, this requires many assumptions that, if not tested correctly, may impact the solution. This is why many development teams use TDD for implementing the interface.

TDD is just a way of constraining a problem, encapsulating the process of design by using the abstraction of a test, and providing rapid feedback as to how well your design is going. The process essentially gives you a nice way to think about and iteratively do design.

By writing a unit test, the programmers put in writing its assumptions about the specifications. These assumptions are expressed using the arrange-act-assert patterns:

- **Arrange:** Set up the unit under a test.

- **Act:** Exercise the unit under a test, capturing any resulting state.

- **Assert:** Verify the behavior through assertions.

Figure 7.8 shows how TDD is a low-level cycle that overlaps within the three-stage process for turning scenarios into acceptance tests. During this low-level cycle, the programmer writes an (initially failing) unit test that defines a programming abstraction, produces the minimum amount of code to pass that test, and finally refactors the new code to remove duplication. The process is iterated as many times as necessary until each unit is functioning according to the wanted specifications.

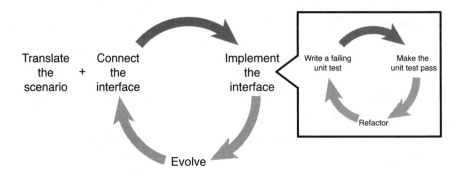

Figure 7.8 *Implementing the interface using TDD.*

Replacing Unit Testing with Context-Specification Testing

For many, the TDD cycle is not about unit testing anymore but rather about specifying the software implementation. These promoters want to improve the language in use in unit tests so that instead of "testing" they are defining "behavior" of a component at the unit level. To achieve this goal, they are replacing their unit testing framework with a context-specification testing framework.

Context-specification testing is just a syntactic difference, not necessarily a different style of testing. It still relies on TDD. However, when writing a unit test, these frameworks replace the arrange-act-assert nomenclature with a vocabulary more appropriate for defining "behavior." For the programmers, this syntactic change matters because it enables them to incrementally build up context. A context can be set up for a test, and some assertions can be performed against that context. Context-specification testing enables the development team to build maintainable software where the behaviors (and the assumptions) can easily be understood several years later, after the original programmers are gone.

Some of the best-known context-specification testing frameworks are RSpec [8] for the Ruby language, JDave [9] for the Java platform, and NSpec [10] for the Microsoft .NET platform.

Making the Test Pass

One of the most overlooked benefits of automating confirmation with acceptance tests is the following—the development team has a precise definition of when it is done implementing a scenario. This definition is not only explicit but also highly visible; this is when the acceptance test turns green.

Making the acceptance test pass is a way to communicate to all involved that the requirements for a particular scenario have been met. It is at that precise moment when the test turns green that the stakeholders' desirements become a requirement. From now on, this acceptance test must always pass. Every new increment must satisfy this acceptance test; otherwise, this is a proof of incongruities with the specifications.

Evolving the Acceptance Test

The *refactor stage* is where the team improves the initial implementation of the software. The aim is to improve the inner workings of the test to remove duplication and reduce technical debt. Instead of making changes in one big chunk, the team should take advantage of the calibrated test to guide programming and ensure a quality result. Here's how it should work. By taking small steps, and making one change at a time, the programmers rearrange the code, always making sure the test responds positively after each little refactoring.

When you reach this last stage of the development cycle, you are no longer specifying the software but rather deeply involved in the implementation. The major difference from the traditional approach is that improvements are done in small refactoring segments, using the passing test (green indicator) as a guide for reaching success.

Running Acceptance Tests Side-by-Side with Continuous Integration

As soon as you start the red-green-refactor cycle, one of the most important engineering practices is to execute the acceptance tests on a recurring basis with the help of an automated build and testing environment. The testing environment is needed to replicate the infrastructure required to accurately test the "executable" scenarios.

You might think that the most sensible approach would be to reuse the continuous integration (CI) environment. CI is a practice in which isolated changes made by developers are immediately tested and reported on when they are committed to the version control. The goal of CI is to provide rapid feedback so that if an integration defect is introduced into the code base, it can be identified and corrected as soon as possible. Because CI detects integration deficiencies early in development, defects are generally smaller, less complex, and easier to solve.

You must resist this temptation to mix acceptance tests with continuous integration. Because of hardware constraints, this can unduly slow down the code integration. CI feedbacks must be fast; otherwise, developers lose interest. Furthermore, developers are not required to check the evolution of the specifications as frequently as the code.

In contrast, confirming acceptance tests only at the end of the sprint is not any better. It would take too long to get feedback on problems with the specifications, making it difficult to correct them.

As a minimum, daily confirmation is what you should aim for. Testing the "executable" scenarios during the nightly build ensures that every morning the team can easily confirm that the software under construction still meets the evolving specifications.

If hardware constraints and budget limitation is not an issue, try to keep pace with CI and have multiple feedback loops during the day by running acceptance tests as a slave build triggered by the CI result.

Even if there are close links between acceptance testing and CI, you must isolate acceptance testing from other testing environments. Create a build script expressly for this task, and run this build script on its own environment. By executing acceptance tests in a specific environment, you can easily retrieve results and publish them.

Enhancing Scenarios with Test Results

This chapter has shown you how to turn scenarios into acceptance tests through automation. All this work was done with one goal in mind: to easily identify which previously successful tests are now failing. You can reach this goal by analyzing raw test results, but it is limiting.

Because it provides context, aggregating results with the specification is much more powerful than just publishing the raw tests results. These combined results enable both the team and the stakeholders to easily visualize quality compliance and work completeness.

Figure 7.9 demonstrates how to enhance scenarios with test results. You use three color schemes to specify the test automation results. The yellow scenarios are pending tests. Yellow states that the specification is completed and that you are now pending implementation. Implemented tests are either green or red. Green means that the scenario is implemented and the test passes, whereas red indicates that the test fails. What matters most are the failing tests highlighted in red. This helps the team visualize conformance to specifications. By highlighting in red the failing scenarios, the team can react quickly and fix the failing tests before proceeding.

Feature: Shopping Cart

Scenario

Given the buyer is logged as a student
When the buyer requests the list of transit fares
Then

Id	Name	Price
002	Student monthly pass	76
100	One day pass	6
202	Student booklet of 10 single tickets	15

Pending Implementation

Scenario

Given an empty shopping cart is created
And a monthly student pass is added to shopping cart
When the buyer checks out the shopping cart
Then a 76 dollar sale occurs

Passed

Scenario

Given an empty shopping cart is created
And a monthly student pass is added to shopping cart
When the buyer removes all items from shopping cart
Then all items are removed from shopping cart

Fail

Figure 7.9 *Visualizing specifications conformance by identifying failing tests.*

Identifying a decline in quality is important but there is more. Tracking and monitoring the work is as important. The main work of the team consists of turning scenarios into acceptance tests that pass. As such, the number of completed tests that turn green is a good unit for measuring the progress of the work.

As shown in Figure 7.10, you can use a burn-down chart to trace completed work and predict whether the team can honor its plan. A burn-down chart is a graphical representation of work left to do, versus time. Every day during the sprint, you add a bar to the graph and split the number of scenarios according to the status of the test results. Only scenarios with a "green" passing test are considered "done." Failing tests, as well as tests pending implementation, represent the amount of work still left to do. In Figure 7.10, there are seven days completed out of a three-week sprint. The blue line crossing the chart represents the downward trend of the actual work "done" during the iteration. Ideally, the chart illustrates a decreasing trend until it "burns down" to zero.

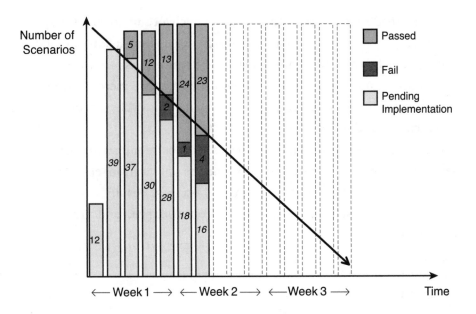

Figure 7.10 *Tracing work completeness by measuring passing tests.*

Summary

This chapter sought to explain how to automate confirmation, or said differently, how to evolve scenarios into acceptance tests. It began by reminding you that a scenario becomes an acceptance test when it is executed. An acceptance test is only a copy of a scenario in a format suitable for execution on a computer. As such, to confirm the same specification, the scenario and its associated test must express the same intent without any distortion.

You learned that turning a scenario into an acceptance test is a three-stage process similar to the red-green-refactor cycle popularized by Test-Driven Development practices. Writing tests first helps to synchronize the development team's assumptions early and to validate whether the implementation is correct for the scenario's assumptions.

You learned that this red-green-refactor cycle occurs during the sprint repeatedly and on a regular basis. Actually, this is how a software increment is built by the development team. The team translates the scenario into an acceptance test, connects it with the software increment, implements the software increment, and evolves it. This cycle is repeated for each scenario and for each user story.

You have learned that "executable" scenarios require a test environment that is different from the continuous integration environment. In addition, this chapter demonstrated how test results can enhance scenarios, help visualize specifications conformance, and trace work completeness.

References

[1]   Beck, Kent. (2002). *Test Driven Development: By Example.* Boston, MA: Addison-Wesley.

[2]   Fowler, Martin. (2010). *Domain-Specific Languages.* Boston, MA: Addison-Wesley.

[3]   http://cukes.info/

[4]   http://jbehave.org/

[5]   http://www.specflow.org/

[6]   http://storyq.codeplex.com/

[7]   Fowler, Martin. (2002). *Patterns of Enterprise Application Architecture.* Boston, MA: Addison-Wesley.

[8]   http://rspec.info/

[9]   http://jdave.org/

[10] http://nspec.tigris.org/

Chapter 8

Addressing Nonfunctional Requirements

A common challenge when specifying software is how to assess the expected quality. Many stakeholders like to believe that quality is implicit and emerges without any special effort. Unfortunately, this is rarely the case. First, what is meant by quality? Crosby's work is definitely the place to start when you try to get a simple definition of quality. In *Quality Is Free* [1], Crosby defines quality as "conformance to requirements," and this has become the standard definition of quality—not just in software development, but universally across all industries. As stated by Crosby, quality is closely linked to requirements. And like requirements, which are covered extensively in this book, what drives quality is difficult to articulate. Wikipedia noted in the article on quality in business, engineering, and manufacturing that "quality is a perceptual, conditional and somewhat subjective attribute and may be understood differently by different people" [2]. This explains why Gerald Weinberg, in his book *Quality Software Management: Systems Thinking* [3], coined the following definition: "Quality is value to some person." This definition emphasizes that quality is inherently subjective and that different people experience the quality of the same software in different ways. Faced with numerous inconsistent viewpoints, it is easy for the development team to focus only on the functional quality and ignore the inner structural quality of the solution.

You saw in the first chapters of this book how to address functional quality through iterative discovery of stakeholders' desirements. Functional quality can be described as "fitness for purpose." This chapter concerns the other side of quality, nonfunctional requirements.

Nonfunctional requirements, also known as technical requirements, quality attributes, or quality of service requirements, enforce the structural quality of the software and define how functional requirements are supposed to be. In contrast with functional requirements, they are not about how to deliver new features, but rather about desirable characteristics of the software. These characteristics include usability, reliability, maintainability, security, portability, testability, and many others. As you can see from that list, nonfunctional requirements are often referred to as "-ilities" because of the suffix many of the words share. Obviously, some nonfunctional requirements do not end in "-ility" such as correctness, performance, robustness, and so on.

Nonfunctional is probably a misnomer because it sounds like they are intangible properties. However, these quality requirements affect the operation of the software, and it is possible to ensure they are present. Dealing improperly with nonfunctional requirements leads to software that cannot evolve or software with displeasing execution qualities. These quality requirements can be divided into two main categories:

1. **External** quality such as performance, reliability, correctness, scalability, robustness, security, and usability, which carry out the software's functions at run time, and as such, is not only visible to stakeholders but is also highly desirable.

2. **Internal** quality such as maintainability, modifiability, and testability, which are barely visible to stakeholders but simplify how to build and evolve the software.

A nonfunctional requirement specifies "how well" the "What" must behave. It imposes constraints that typically cut across functional requirements. As such, it defines a restriction to be obeyed either during the implementation by the team (internal quality) or at run time by the software (external quality). It limits the software behavior to satisfy stakeholders.

Addressing nonfunctional requirements is what you learn in this chapter. It explains how to improve external quality using restrictions and how to ensure internal quality during software construction with sound engineering practices.

Improving External Quality Using Restrictions

External quality consists of those highly desirable attributes perceived during the execution of the software by stakeholders. The nonfunctional requirements that affect the external quality are numerous. They are not only highly visible but also rarely requested by stakeholders. However, their absence quickly causes dissatisfaction. Fortunately, not all of them are of equal importance. As shown in Table 8.1, there are eight requirements that are most likely to affect the external quality of every application.

Table 8.1   *Nonfunctional Requirements That Most Likely Affect External Quality*

Name	Definition
Accessibility	Ease with which the software can be accessed by as many people as possible.
Correctness	Capability of the software with respect to matching or meeting the specification.
Performance	Ease with which the software does the work it is supposed to do. Usually it is measured as a response time or a throughput.
Reliability	Capability of the software to perform its required functions under stated conditions for a specified period of time.
Robustness	Capability of the software to cope with errors during execution.
Scalability	Capability of the software to handle growing amounts of work in a graceful manner.
Security	Degree to which the software protects against threats.
Usability	Ease with which the software can be used by specified users to achieve specified goals.

Ignoring those eight nonfunctional requirements is one of the shortcomings found abundantly in many software applications. Experience shows that inefficiency, or absence of any of these nonfunctional requirements, generates stakeholders' dissatisfaction and can lead to failure. The lack of expertise regarding architecture partly explains this situation, but there is more. Nonfunctional requirements affect the entire system, and it is difficult to isolate them. In addition, they are a recurring concern, so it is easy to worry about them on an occasional basis and then ignore them in future sprints.

The development team must accomplish sufficient, but not excessive, architectural work early on and build on it throughout the life of the software. The issue is so critical that teams should formalize the role of the architect and ensure that at least one team member takes ownership of this role. Just like the product owner trawls desirements incrementally, step by step, using a vision-centric and an emergent iterative practice, the architect specifies an emergent architecture in two ways:

- By addressing nonfunctional requirements in small chunks and in a timely manner
- By designing technical abstractions through thoughtful reduction and organization

The architect leads the design of the structural foundation upon which the solution is built by the team. This leadership is not done in isolation. The architect works collaboratively with every team member to remove accidental complexity and pursues simplicity in the design.

Even though the role of the architect is more than just correctly addressing quality attributes, this remains one of the most visible areas of his work. It would be presumptuous to believe that all the knowledge required to satisfy the many nonfunctional requirements could be summarized in a few pages. The know-how someone needs to have to meet each of these "ilities" can easily fill many books. Furthermore, learning to master the nonfunctional requirements is a skill that architects acquire with experience.

This book aims to achieve a much simpler goal. You should translate nonfunctional requirements into restrictions and make them explicit knowledge shared by the whole team. A factor often underestimated is that explicit and highly visible elements are always taken into consideration by the team. As such, restrictions are the visible elements that guide the work and help determine whether the team has satisfied the nonfunctional requirements. Satisfying the restrictions not only makes stakeholders happier, but also helps to build trust and improve the quality of future conversations.

Translating Nonfunctional Requirements into Restrictions

The most common mistake when specifying software is the lack of a clearly defined set of restrictions that summarize the required quality. A restriction imposes conditions that set a limit to comply with. Like any other specification element, each restriction should be clear, simple, and understandable. A great way to ensure this is to use the SMART principle first written up by Mike Mannion and Barry Keepence [1]. Basically, the SMART principle suggests that a restriction should be each of the following:

- Specific: It should target a piece of functionality that is small, consistent, and simple.

- Measurable: It imposes a limit that is measurable; otherwise, how would you know when you've addressed it?

- Attainable: It is recognized as achievable by the team.

- Relevant: It is directly related, connected, and pertinent to the nonfunctional requirement.

- Traceable: It is linked with a functional requirement that justifies why it exists.

Explicitly setting restrictions is a simple and obvious step to start with. This simplifies the design by setting a goal that will be recognized and shared by the whole team. When this first step is done correctly, those restrictions can guide the team to successfully address nonfunctional requirements.

Should You Express Nonfunctional Requirements as User Stories?

Expressing non-functional requirements as user stories is certainly not my first choice. The main reason is stories are placeholders for functional requirements. They are not a good artifact for expressing restrictions that impose constraints. They convey a vague functional scope to evaluate what needs to be restricted. The "What" that needs to be restricted is not concrete enough because the scope of a story is the iteration it belongs to. In addition, if you want to make sure not to induce technical debt once the story is completed, you must put it back in the backlog to make it available for a future sprint. This unduly complicates the management of the backlog.

Having clarified my reluctance in this matter, there are nonetheless cases where it makes sense to define a restriction with a user story. Let's say a non-functional requirement such as globalization, which had initially been considered insignificant, suddenly becomes a concern. For example, suppose that a new business acquisition forces the team to evolve the software to support multiple languages. Since this change needs to be applied system-wide, it is advisable to specify the new restriction as a story (and probably slice it into smaller sub-stories when it is close to being delivered).

Because it imposes conditions that set a limitation, the team can easily misinterpret a restriction as an attempt to reduce what should be delivered. On the other hand, a well-defined restriction is intended to fix the limits within which you are free, empowered, and challenged to innovate. A limiting restriction offers a unique opportunity for growth and innovation. The idea of operating within boundaries—of making more with less—is especially relevant when you specify as you go, by writing a small chunk of requirements using an emergent iterative practice. When you have fewer options, it is much easier to design a technical solution that satisfies what is desired. The imposition of limits doesn't stifle creativity—it enables it.

The most important element of a restriction is the *measure*. It is well known that if you can't measure it, you won't know when you've achieved it. The challenge when expressing a measure is to reduce the scale of what needs to be measured. In the case of nonfunctional requirements, a measure is much more specific and easier to express if you reduce the functional scope. This is why applying the restriction to a simple and specific functional scope is important.

Reducing the Functional Scope to a Single Scenario

To effectively translate a nonfunctional requirement into a restriction, you must ensure that the restriction is intertwined with a simple piece of functionality. As shown in Figure 8.1, whenever possible, you should apply a restriction to a single scenario. Because of their simplicity, scenarios, which are used to confirm user stories, are the perfect artifact for imposing a restriction.

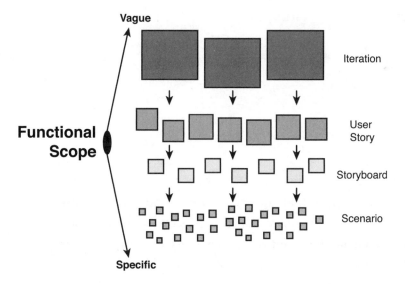

Figure 8.1 *Imposing restrictions using a concrete and specific functional scope.*

Unlike a nonfunctional requirement, which is a recurrent concern, a restriction is self-contained and can be satisfied in a finite period of time. As shown in Figure 8.2, a restriction is addressed side by side with its linked scenario.

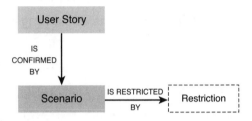

Figure 8.2 *Addressing a restriction side by side with its linked functional scope.*

As shown in Figure 8.3, you should never link a restriction directly with a user story. Stories provide a vague context and are not specific enough to efficiently guide the team during implementation. Always link the restriction with a scenario.

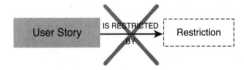

Figure 8.3 *Avoid linking restrictions with a user story.*

During each sprint, the team looks at the scenarios to identify the non-functional requirements that must be enforced and creates restrictions to address it. Figure 8.4 shows that this process is repeated story after story. The scenarios that confirm a user story are formally completed only when all the restrictions are fully inventoried.

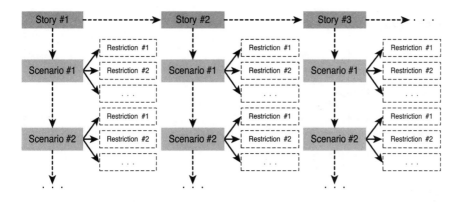

Figure 8.4 *Linking restrictions with scenarios is a process repeated story after story.*

In addition to linking the restriction with a clear-cut functional scope, the scenario is now much more concrete and provides an easily measurable quality objective.

Setting Measurable Quality Objectives

As said previously, a restriction must be measurable. By setting explicit quality objectives, the restriction sets a measurable goal that the development team should verify. A restriction imposes conditions and sets a limit that the software needs to comply with during execution. It describes a significant desire that is required for the fulfillment of the scenario. This is an instance serving to illustrate highly appealing outcomes for stakeholders.

Figure 8.5 shows how a restriction enhances a scenario and sets a measurable quality objective to be met.

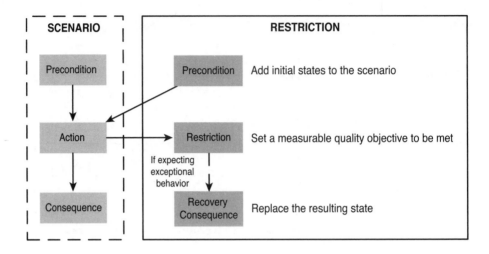

Figure 8.5 *Enhancing a scenario with a restriction.*

A restriction expresses a "measurable" constraint to add to a scenario. This constraint contains a precondition, a restriction, and if necessary, a recovery consequence. A precondition is used to add supplementary initial states to a scenario. The restriction is the explicit quality objective that must be met after the scenario is completed. If the restriction expresses exceptional behavior, the recovery consequence is the new resulting state. If there is no exceptional behavior, the recovery consequence is omitted and the normal consequence, defined initially within the scenario, occurs.

The goal in this chapter is not only to familiarize you with restrictions, but also to provide a precise language in which to express them. It should be noted that the syntax proposed in the following paragraphs is not available in the current BDD automation frameworks. This syntax is a pure creation, a proposal that hopefully will be adopted in the coming years by the tool makers.

By adding simple keywords similar to the Given-When-Then syntax, you can express restrictions with formality. These keywords help improve not only communication among people, but within software tooling as well.

The syntax is expressed as follows:

```
Given one precondition
   And another precondition
   And yet another precondition
Restrict after x occurrence with a measurable quality
objective
Then a consequence
   And another consequence
```

Each clause is described in the following:

Given: The additional and necessary preconditions to put the scenario in a known state to exercise the restriction.

Restrict: The quality objective to measure after 1 or x occurrences of the scenario. If there is only one occurrence the after 1 occurrence can be omitted. There should be only one Restrict clause per restriction.

Then: The consequence that occurs if exercising the restriction creates exceptional behavior. This is the observable outcome of the system.

And: It is a placeholder that replaces "Given" or "Then" clauses when there are several of them.

Let's demonstrate this syntax with a concrete example. Imagine that you want to express a restriction for the following scenario as defined in Figure 8.6.

Table

ShoppingCart.Fixtures.ListOfStudentFares		
Id	Name	Price
001	Single Ticket	$1.50
002	Booklet of 10 Single tickets	$9.75
003	1-Day Card	$4.00
004	3-Day Card	$11.00
005	Weekly Pass	$15.00
006	Monthly Pass	$76.00

Given-When-Then

```
Given the buyer is a student
When the buyer requests the list of fares
Then response is
  | Id  | Name                        | Price   |
  | 001 | Single Ticket               | $1.50   |
  | 002 | Booklet of 10 Single tickets| $9.75   |
  | 003 | 1-Day Card                  | $4.00   |
  | 004 | 3-Day Card                  | $11.00  |
  | 005 | Weekly Pass                 | $15.00  |
  | 006 | Monthly Pass                | $76.00  |
```

Figure 8.6 *Querying a list of items in a scenario.*

Here is the simplest restriction that you could write:

```
Restrict with response time less than 5 seconds
```

Usually, restrictions are more complex. This is the case when expressing the happy path of a restriction; you will add not only the "Restrict" clause but also a "Given" clause to add a new precondition:

```
Given the buyer is user 'KnownBuyer'
Restrict with the buyer to be authenticated positively
```

Similarly, when expressing exceptional behavior that replaces the normal consequence of the scenario you can add a "Then" clause:

```
Given the buyer is user 'UnknownBuyer'
Restrict with the buyer to be authenticated negatively
Then issue is saved in security database and user is
redirected to "Login" page
```

Whenever possible, for each quality objective, you should write two restrictions, one that evaluates the happy path and a second that evaluates an unacceptable case. Sometimes, the happy path is unnecessary because it repeats the normal outcomes of the scenario. In this case, only the unacceptable case needs to be made explicit:

```
Given the server is down
Restrict with a query that returns a list of 0 transit fares
Then user is redirected to page "Server unavailable. Please
try later"
```

Each restriction is specific for one scenario. However, sometimes you need to repeat the scenario many times to verify that the restriction is met. Say that you want to set explicit restrictions for scalability. Imagine that the software should not handle more than 10,000 concurrent users. You could express the restriction as this:

```
Restrict after 10001 occurrences with a failed login
Then user is redirected to page "Server unavailable. Please
try later"
```

Always ensure that the quality objective is measurable so that it is easy to evaluate when the restriction fails. For example, if you want to set explicit restrictions for usability, ensure that the criterion for failure is easily recognizable:

```
Restrict after 10 occurrences with 8 users that complete the
scenario by themselves without any human help
```

Obviously, often it is difficult to automate restrictions with an acceptance test. This explains why nothing similar to the syntax I propose is included with existing BDD automation framework. This is a challenge that must be addressed, especially since it is nothing new because software quality teams have been facing it for many years. Fortunately, there are great testing practices for measuring quality. Let's discuss these practices in more detail.

Testing Restrictions with Proven Practices

A test is a verification that aims to find a maximum number of problematic behaviors within a software application. It is the method of choice for verifying restrictions. Restrictions illustrate the nonfunctional requirements. They confirm quality objectives. Table 8.2 presents a list of some of the proven practices for testing restrictions.

Table 8.2   *Proven Practices for Testing Restrictions*

Nonfunctional Requirement	Testing Practice
Accessibility	Verify visual impairments, mobility difficulty, hearing inability, and cognitive disabilities.
Correctness	Determine whether the software respects the specification (acceptance testing).
Performance	Measure response time and inspect throughput.
Reliability	Seek extraordinary resource consumption over a specified period of time (memory, CPU, and disk space).
Robustness	Determine the capability of the software to function correctly in the presence of invalid inputs or stressful environmental conditions (stress testing).
Scalability	Verify software behavior under both normal and anticipated peak load conditions (load testing).
Security	Perform intrusion detection and vulnerability scanning.
Usability	Conduct heuristic evaluations, consistency inspections, and activity analyses to verify whether users have achieved their specified goals.

Confirming restrictions with these proven practices can be expensive in terms of effort. As is often the case when tackling complex requirements, experience shows that less is more. You should always negotiate with stakeholders to reduce the number of restrictions. Question every nonfunctional requirement to validate whether it is actually a desirable outcome. If possible, try to transform a quality attribute from a recurrent concern to a one-time concern that will be addressed in a specific sprint. This substantially reduces the workload because you handle the concern as a user story in only one specific sprint.

Nonfunctional requirements can easily endanger the successful completion of the sprint because often we underestimate the work to be done. Confirming restrictions is a difficult task, mainly because the development team can test only by executing a full version of the software. Complete software is rarely available early in the sprint. The product owner must be prepared to receive requests from the development team to lower restrictions as the team progresses in the sprint.

The simplest approach, when reducing restrictions, is to make visible to the stakeholders the costs involved in satisfying the restriction. Explain the issues and look for less expensive alternatives. An inexpensive option, at least in the short term, is to defer the need and meet the restriction in a future sprint. However, be aware that this is not desirable. Deferring the meeting of a restriction can lead to a large amount of reworking in future sprints, due to architectural considerations. If deferring remains your decision, be sure not to lose track of the initial nonfunctional requirement by creating and storing in the backlog a story/scenario that specifically targets the unmet restriction.

Although it is always feasible to relax restrictions for the external quality, things are highly different for the internal quality. This is what the next section discusses.

Ensuring Internal Quality Using Sound Engineering Practices

When dealing with software construction, the team must "always" deliver a sprint with enough internal quality so that it can easily continue to extend it in future iterations. If the nonfunctional requirements that affect the internal quality are successfully met, the software under construction is not only simplified, but its sustainability is also preserved for future changes. As shown in Table 8.3, the list of nonfunctional requirements that are most likely affecting the internal quality is rather short.

Table 8.3 *Nonfunctional Requirements That Are Most Likely Affecting the Internal Quality*

Name	Definition
Simplicity	Ease of understanding or explaining
Maintainability	Ease of changing and evolving with minimal effort
Testability	Ease of confirming conformance by observing a reproducible behavior
Portability	Ease of reuse for multiple platforms
Extensibility	Ease of taking into consideration future growth

As said previously, this chapter doesn't show how to achieve an acceptable level of internal quality. It is usually the type of know-how expected from a developer and is beyond the scope of this book. However, sound engineering practices to ensure the software construction is done correctly are described.

Improving Software Construction with Explicit Practices

Without proven practices, programmers can hardly work to maximize nonfunctional requirements. Practices provide an operational framework for ensuring that the software construction is done correctly. For example, applying self-documenting code is a well-known engineering practice for achieving simplicity.

Self-documenting code: Practice of ensuring code is its own best documentation by enabling useful information, such as programming constructs and logical structure, to be deduced from the naming convention and code layout convention.

Practices are intimately linked with the Definition of Done checklist. The Definition of Done checklist consists of the current practices and standards of the team. This is the checklist team members complete when producing software. When looking at examples of Definition of Done in various teams, they usually include points like

- Code completed.
- 0 (known) bugs.
- Passed unit tests.
- Code peer-reviewed or paired.
- Code checked in.
- Deployed to test environment and passed tests.
- Documentation updated.

Just as the team should clarify what "Done" means, it must also identify early on which practices will guide the work. The benefits of having an explicit set of practices is that after it is defined, the team can apply those practices, story after story, sprint after sprint. This means that the team needs to identify and specify the practices only once. From time to time, however, practices should be revised in response to retrospective and continuous improvement, just like with the Definition of Done.

Start small and choose proven practices first. Table 8.4 presents a list of well-known practices in widespread usage.

Table 8.4 *Key Practices to Apply When Programming*

Nonfunctional Requirement	Practice
Simplicity	**Self-documenting code:** Practice of ensuring code is its own best documentation by enabling useful information, such as programming constructs and logical structure, to be deduced from the naming convention and code layout convention.
	Code metrics: Practice of measuring the complexity of the source code to provide developers better insight into the quality of the code they are producing.
Maintainability	**Continuous integration:** Practice in which isolated changes made by developers are immediately tested and reported on when they are committed to the version control.
	Branching and merging: Practice of merging source code from the development branch with the main branch (and tagging appropriately for traceability).
Testability	**Red-green-refactor:** Design practice of translating into a test the assumptions about the externally visible behavior of the abstraction to implement, then calibrating test by making it fail (red) and pass (green), and then implementing using feedbacks from the calibrated test to comply with the initial assumptions (refactor).
	Code coverage: Practice of measuring the degree to which the source code has been tested.
Portability	**Multitarget compiling:** Practice of verifying that the integrated code can be compiled on every platform.

Though we may have the good fortune to implement sound engineering practices that provide clear targets for the team, they are of little use if not applied. In contrast to the external quality, you can hardly postpone the work required to ensure simplicity, maintainability, testability, or portability. Postponing creates a technical debt that can cripple the team's ability to add new functionality. It is therefore important for the team to master the engineering practices and apply them on a daily basis.

Should You Care About Extensibility?

Extensibility is an internal quality rarely required by stakeholders. Historically, in a plan-driven organization, the role of software architects was to conceive the overall solution using a big upfront design. It is therefore not a surprise that many architects love to anticipate future needs.

Unfortunately, often our experience indicates that future growth proves extensibility requirements are nonexistent. Too many teams consider fictitious extensibility requirements at the expense of the stakeholders' immediate needs. The agile community uses the acronym YAGNI which means "You ain't gonna need it" to express that you should add capabilities only when you actually need them, never when you just foresee that you need them. Extensibility requires the team to anticipate and predict the future, which is precisely what we refuse to do with agile software development. This is significant because whatever you build upfront, as a response to an anticipated future, will have to be refactored to fit the final requirements. This will prove more expensive. In conclusion, extensibility is a nonfunctional requirement that is largely overrated.

Mastering Practices with Collaborative Construction

Collaborative construction refers to techniques in which teammates share responsibility for creating code and other artifacts. It is the simplest way to ensure that engineering practices are successfully applied and mastered. Two collaborative construction techniques widely used are collective code ownership and pair programming.

Collective code ownership requires that all teammates ensure software quality and share responsibility for maintaining the source code. Anyone can make necessary changes anywhere, and everyone is expected to apply refactoring when problems or improvements are found. To make this work, teammates must let go of their egos. They must take as much pride in the team's shared code as in their own code.

Collective code ownership requires discipline and is usually successful when applied, side by side, with pair programming.

Pair programming is a technique in which two teammates work together at one workstation: the driver, typing at the keyboard, and the observer, verifying what is produced. The two teammates switch roles frequently. While reviewing, the observer also considers the constraints imposed by the practices. The observer's main contribution is to come up with ideas for improvements and identify potential problems. This enables the driver to focus his attention on the task at hand, using the observer as a safety net and guide.

Pairing does not require adopting an all-or-nothing approach. Not all the source code should be written in pair programming; only a subset should be done in pairing according to selection criteria. For example, a team could decide to work in pairs only one hour per day. Another option is to put into place rules for pairing when an event occurs indicating poor quality such as

- Check-in breaks the continuous integration.
- Code metric such as cyclomatic complexity is too high during the last check-in.

Pair programming may initially appear both compelling and disturbing. One certainty is that it requires change to the work process. However, the radical change in the way work is produced with pair programming sends a strong signal to team members on the willingness of the organization to produce learning teams with continuous process improvement. Moreover, in addition to promoting the proper use of engineering practices, pairing can also act as defect-detection techniques during construction. Pairing not only tends to find different kinds of errors, it also finds a higher percentage of defects than testing [4].

Summary

This chapter explained how to address nonfunctional requirements, or said differently, how to deliver quality software. You were reminded that the required quality can be divided into two main categories:

1. **External** quality is how well the software carries out its functions at run time, and as such, is not only visible to stakeholders, but is also highly desirable.

2. **Internal** quality is characteristics of the software barely visible to stakeholders but which simplifies the process of building and evolving the software.

A nonfunctional requirement specifies "how well" the "What" must behave. It imposes constraints that typically cut across functional requirements. As such, it defines a restriction to be obeyed either during the implementation by the team (internal quality) or at run time by the software (external quality). It limits the software behavior to satisfy stakeholders.

You have learned to improve external quality by translating nonfunctional requirements into restrictions. A restriction expresses a "measurable" constraint to add to a scenario. We have explained how to express restrictions with formality using simple keywords similar to the Given-When-Then syntax. A factor often underestimated is that explicit and highly visible elements are always taken into consideration by the team. As such, restrictions are the visible elements that guide the work and help determine whether the team has satisfied the nonfunctional requirements.

In the last section of this chapter, you learned how to improve internal quality during software construction by using sound engineering practices. Proven practices, such as self-documenting code, continuous integration, and red-green-refactor were presented. We concluded by explaining that collaborative construction techniques, such as collective code ownership and pair programming, are the easiest ways to ensure development teams apply these practices.

References

[1]   Crosby, Philip B. (1979). *Quality Is Free: The Art of Making Quality Certain*. Columbus, OH: McGraw-Hill.

[2]   http://en.wikipedia.org/wiki/Quality_(business)

[3]   Weinberg, Gerald M. (1991). *Quality Software Management: Systems Thinking*. New York, NY: Dorset House.

[4]   Begel, Andrew, Nachiappan Nagappan (2008). "Pair Programming: What's in it for Me?" http://research.microsoft.com/pubs/75108/esem-begel-2008.pdf

Chapter 9

Conclusion

We've all heard our parents or teachers repeat this famous quote, hoping to make us persevere when faced with a problem: "Whatever is worth doing at all is worth doing well." Now that years have passed and we are wiser, there is plenty to learn from this quote. At first glance, the vast majority of us will understand this quote as "If you are going to put time and effort into solving a problem, solve it right." Only after careful consideration can we discover a second perspective that is just as important; "If you are going to put time and effort into solving a problem, ensure that you first solve the right problem and then that you solve it properly." This book is all about the second perspective. It aims to solve the paramount challenge encountered by many software development teams: They do not build the right software.

This book presented a compendium of the agile practices related to executable specifications. Executable specifications enable you to automatically test the behavior of the software against the specifications so that the development team can ensure that it solves the right problem before solving it right. As explained throughout this book, working with executable specifications is not merely a simple recipe, but rather a mindset. To be successful, you must remember that above all else, needs are emergent and constantly evolving. There is no set plan that can and will be successful. Instead, it is a question of constantly being open to changes and uncertainties. It is only when flexibility is embraced that the proper attitude can be taken.

Recapitulating the Book

As indicated in Chapter 1, "Solving the Right Problem," even with the best intentions, you cannot force agreement upon stakeholders. Keep the following African proverb in mind, "You can't make grass grow faster by pulling on it." When requirements are difficult to grasp and are in constant flux, teams should not rely on requirements gathering inherited from traditional engineering. To deal with these uncertainties, teams should adopt empirical techniques based on an agile requirements discovery and accept that nothing is ever fully stable or predictable.

In Chapter 2, "Relying on a Stable Foundation," you learned that before moving forward, it is important to clarify the things that will hardly change. This stable foundation can establish a shared vision of the solution and simplify the iterative requirements discovery.

Chapter 3, "Discovering Through Short Feedback Loops and Stakeholders' Desirements," showed that to tackle uncertainties, you must learn to discover stakeholders' desirements. A desirement is a discrete piece of demonstrable functionality that stakeholders desire and perceive as a requirement. The importance of approaching such a challenge with an open mind by using the trial-and-error principle in the form of frequent feedback loops was stressed.

As delineated in Chapter 4, "Expressing Desirements with User Stories," you learned how to express desirements with user stories and how to record them using the product backlog. The product backlog is an ordered list where the accumulation of user stories is recorded. A user story is a short description written in everyday language using the classic template "As a <role>, I want <desire> so that <benefit>." By decoupling roles, desires, and benefits, user stories establish a ubiquitous language that enforces a shared understanding.

Chapter 5, "Refining User Stories by Grooming the Product Backlog," explained that to groom the product backlog, you must rank, illustrate, size, and split user stories. You learned the importance of having a product owner: someone who not only leads backlog grooming but also ensures that it is done in collaboration with stakeholders and the development team. This chapter demonstrated how to use collaboration boards to track the user stories' evolution during the grooming process. It concluded by explaining that when a story has gone through the process of grooming, you have reached an important milestone, which is the transition from conversation to confirmation. Confirmation conveys additional information about the story and establishes the success criteria. Within the context of executable specifications, you can confirm success criteria with scenarios. Scenarios say, in the words of the stakeholders, how they expect to verify the desirable outcome. As such, scenarios enable the team to know when the story is done.

Chapter 6, "Confirming User Stories with Scenarios," demonstrated how scenarios confirm user stories by scripting behaviors in a formal way. You learned that confirming stories is a two-step process. Initially, you start by specifying only the storyboard and the key scenarios. Subsequently, when a story is planned by the team for delivery, you finalize all the scenarios during a specification workshop. The specification workshop brings together, at the beginning of the sprint, the team and stakeholders to create a shared understanding of all the scenarios to be delivered during the sprint.

It was not until Chapter 7, "Automating Confirmation with Acceptance Tests," that the executable portion of the specification was discussed. It explained how to transform specifications in a format suitable for execution on a computer by turning scenarios into automated acceptance tests. These acceptance tests enable the development team to easily confirm the behavior of the software against the evolving specifications. Transforming a scenario into an acceptance test is a three-stage process similar to the red-green-refactor cycle popularized by Test-Driven Development practices. The team translates the scenario into an acceptance test, connects it with the software increment, implements the software increment, and evolves it. This cycle is repeated for each scenario and for each user story. Writing tests first helps to synchronize the development team assumptions early and to validate whether the implementation is correct, for the scenario's assumptions.

Finally, Chapter 8 concluded this book by teaching you how to specify nonfunctional requirements, or said differently, how to deliver quality software. A nonfunctional requirement specifies "How well" the "What" must behave. It imposes constraints that typically cut across functional requirements. As such, it defines a restriction to be obeyed either during the implementation by the team (internal quality) or at run time by the software (external quality). You have learned to improve external quality by translating nonfunctional requirements into restrictions. Similarly, you learned how to improve internal quality during software construction by using sound engineering practices.

Summarizing the Process

Figure 9.1 summarizes how the process proposed in this book fits within the Scrum framework. First, backlog grooming, which consists of ranking, illustrating, sizing, and splitting user stories, is a set of events that take place side-by-side to the sprint. Second, at the beginning of the sprint, prior to the sprint planning, the specifications workshop helps to clarify the scenario to be delivered during the sprint. Third, the repetitive cycle of translating, connecting, implementing, and evolving scenarios into automated tests occurs during the sprint. This cycle does not interfere with the daily scrum but rather confirms the work cycle used by the team.

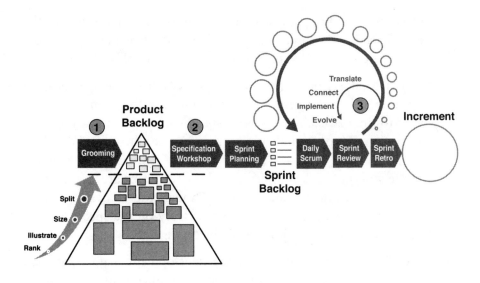

Figure 9.1 *Summarizing the process.*

Drawing Attention to Individual Roles

Even the best process is nothing without a team with complementary skills linked to a common purpose. To ensure team members operate with a high degree of interdependence, share responsibility for self-management, and are accountable for the collective performance, their roles in the team must be crystal clear.

Team members must take on various roles to ensure executable specifications are correctly specified and implemented. There are five major responsibilities in any team applying executable specifications: the product owner, the analyst, the tester, the programmer, and the architect.

- **Product owner:** Product owner is the most visible role because it is the only one assigned to a specific individual. The product owner is the primary interface between the development team and the stakeholders. He is the definitive authority on all that concerns specifications. Though on a day-to-day basis, the product owner manages and prioritizes the backlog, one of his fundamental responsibilities is to carry the overall vision of the software. The product owner understands the big picture and, as such, is truly the bearer of the vision. Faced with the unexpected, the product owner knows how to stay the course and is responsive to the stakeholders' changes.

- **Analyst:** Analysts begin their work as a result of the specification workshop. They are responsible for fulfilling the many tasks required to finalize each user story's specifications. The analyst's role does not consist of a single individual. As a result, several developers can be named analysts. It is the analysts' responsibility to make sure the storyboard is completed and the scenarios are well defined and thereby ready for automation. Though the analysts are part of the development team, their focus is truly on the specifications. Analysts work closely with the product owner.

- **Tester:** Testers are members of the development team concerned with automating confirmation using acceptance tests. Their main responsibility is to translate scenarios into failing acceptance tests. Testers transpose, using an internal DSL, the Given-When-Then steps of the scenarios into an acceptance test. They calibrate the failing tests by designing and connecting the programming interface.

- **Programmer:** Programmers are developers who are responsible for implementing the software's behavior behind the programming interface. They complete the calibration of the failed acceptance tests by making it successful. The aim is to make the test pass by coding a simple implementation and then evolving it by refactoring.

- **Architect:** Architects are members of the development team who are responsible for designing the structural foundation upon which the solution is built. Their role is to ensure the development team builds the software right and delivers quality work. One of their most important responsibilities is to address nonfunctional requirements. They do this by translating nonfunctional requirements into restrictions, thereby making them accessible to the whole team.

If you want to build the right software, make sure you have the right team. Not only do you need a healthy team with the characteristics described in Chapter 2, but you also need a team with members who will fulfill these five roles. It is common to find a product owner and developers who can fill in the role of programmer or tester, so these roles are rarely an issue. The most frequently absent roles are the architect and analyst. Make sure that some team members wear these hats. Having team members who take turns carrying out the responsibility of architect and analyst is key to achieving success.

Glossary

acceptance test—A copy of a scenario in a format suitable for execution on a computer that runs against the software to confirm that the development team is building the right software and is satisfying stakeholders' desirements.

accessibility—A nonfunctional requirement characterizing the ease with which the software can be accessed by as many people or systems as possible.

action—The behavior performed by a scenario causing a transition to occur. It is the body of the "When" clause in a Given-When-Then scenario.

agile software development—A group of software development frameworks that encourage rapid and flexible response to change. It is based on iterative development where requirements and solutions evolve through customer collaboration. The Manifesto for Agile Software Development introduced the term in 2001.

analyst—A developer responsible for ensuring that the storyboard and scenarios related with a user story and due in a sprint are refined and completed. The responsibility of the analyst is related to the specification and in no way with how the implementation will be accomplished.

architect—A developer responsible for designing the structural foundation upon which the solution is built and for specifying an emergent architecture by addressing nonfunctional requirements in small chunks and in a timely manner.

branching and merging—A practice of merging source code from the development branch with the main branch (and tagging appropriately for traceability).

burn-down chart—A graphical representation of work left to do versus time. It is useful for predicting when all the work will be completed.

code coverage—A practice of measuring the degree to which the source code has been tested.

code metrics—A practice of measuring the complexity of the source code to provide developers with better insight into the quality of the code they produce.

collaboration board—A two-dimensional grid on which you move yellow stickies from column to column to guide the actions of team members. Each column represents a state of the process and each sticky note is a visual signal for guiding the collaboration. The aim is to move each sticky note from state to state to accomplish a workflow through cooperation among teammates.

collective code ownership—A practice of sharing responsibility for maintaining the source code.

command—An action that mutates the state of the software. A command always changes the state of the software.

common goal—A one-line summary that explicitly states why the software must exist from the stakeholders' perspective.

concept—A unit of meaning that expresses the behavior of the problem's domain. Using domain vocabulary, the concept gives a unique name to the precondition states, the action, and consequence states that make up a scenario.

consequence—A resulting state of the scenario. It is the body of the "Then" clause in a Given-When-Then syntax.

continuous integration—A practice in which isolated changes made by developers are immediately tested and reported on when they are committed to the version control.

correctness—A nonfunctional requirement characterizing the capability of the software for matching or meeting the specification.

desire—A discrete piece of demonstrable functionality that is valuable to a stakeholder or a group of stakeholders.

desirement—A request for software to change that stakeholders desire and perceive as a requirement.

definition of "Done"—A checklist of practices and standards team members must complete when producing software.

domain model—A web of interconnected objects that encapsulate the core behaviors to solve problems in a domain.

domain-specific language (DSL)—A computer programming language of limited expressiveness focused on a particular domain. In the context of executable specifications, a DSL is a computer programming language represented within the syntax of the general-purpose language already in use by the team, which focuses on translating a scenario into an acceptance test with the same intent and without any distortion from the original scenario.

executable specification—A repository of stakeholders' desirements expressed as features, user stories, storyboards, scenarios, and acceptance tests in a way suitable for execution on a computer that makes it easy to confirm that the development team is building the right software.

extensibility—A nonfunctional requirement characterizing the ease of taking into consideration future growth.

external quality—The structural characteristics, such as performance, reliability, correctness, scalability, robustness, security, and usability, which carry out the software's functions at run time, and as such, are not only visible to stakeholders but are also highly desirable.

feature—A piece of high-level functionality that delivers value to one or more stakeholders. It is a business activity that separates into several user stories.

feedback loop—A time-box period for deliberate discovery through a rigorous trial-and-error process.

Fibonacci sequence—A sequence of numbers, such as 1, 1, 2, 3, 5, 8, 13..., in which each successive number is equal to the sum of the two preceding numbers.

FIT tabular format—A formalized technique for scripting a scenario by using a simple table that represents the action and causes a transition to occur. The table visually expresses, from left to right, and within columns, the precondition and consequence states that you find in a scenario.

fluent interface—A style of domain-specific language that puts together whole sentences using method chaining. It uses a sequence of method calls where each call acts on the result of the previous calls.

flow—A mental state of operation in which a person performing an activity is fully immersed in a feeling of energized focus, full involvement, and enjoyment in the process of the activity.

functional requirement—A desirable functionality, valuable to a stakeholder or a group of stakeholders.

given-when-then syntax—A formalized technique for scripting a scenario as follows: "Given a precondition, When an action occurs, Then a consequence." The "Given" is the precondition state that must be satisfied before taking action. The "When" is the action causing a transition to occur. The "Then" is the consequence state of the action.

God complex—Refusing to admit the possibility of error or failure, even in the face of complex or intractable problems, or difficult or impossible tasks.

grooming—The act of ranking, illustrating, sizing, and splitting user stories.

internal quality—The structural characteristics, such as maintainability, modifiability and testability, which are barely visible to stakeholders but simplify how to build and evolve the software.

iteration—A short feedback loop during which software is created that enables development teams to inspect and adapt to the stakeholders' changing desirements.

maintainability—A nonfunctional requirement characterizing the ease of changing and evolving.

multitarget compiling—A practice of verifying that the integrated code can be compiled on every platform.

nonfunctional requirement—A desirable characteristic, such as usability, reliability, maintainability, and security that is valuable to a stakeholder or a group of stakeholders and that enforces the internal and external quality of the software and defines how functional requirements are supposed to be.

pair programming—A programming technique in which two teammates work together at one workstation: the driver, typing at the keyboard, and the observer, verifying what is produced.

paper prototype—A low-fidelity storyboarding technique that involves creating hand-sketched drawings of the user interface for the purpose of previsualizing the behavior of a user story.

performance—A nonfunctional requirement characterizing the ease with which the software does the work it is supposed to do. Usually, it is measured as a response time or a throughput.

precondition—The initial state of the scenario before action is taken. It is the body of the "Given" clause in a Given-When-Then syntax.

portability—A nonfunctional requirement characterizing the ease of reuse for multiple platforms.

problem—A difference between things as desired and things as perceived.

product backlog—An ordered list that records stakeholders' desirements and describes the "What" that will be built, sorted by importance.

product owner—A team member who is the primary interface between the development team and the stakeholders. The product owner is the definitive authority on all that concerns specifications. His main responsibility is to decide the ordering of what will be built and list these decisions into the product backlog.

programmer—A developer responsible for implementing the software's behavior behind the programming interface. Programmers complete the calibration of the failed acceptance tests by making it successful. The aim is to make the test pass by coding a simple implementation and after that to evolve it using refactoring.

quality—A perceived conformance to requirements.

query—An action that reads the state of the software and returns a data-centric response. A query never changes the state of the software.

red/green/refactor cycle—A design practice of translating into a test the assumptions about the externally visible behavior of the abstraction to implement, then calibrating the test by making it fail (red) and pass (green), and then implementing by using feedbacks from the calibrated test to comply with the initial assumptions (refactor).

reliability—A nonfunctional requirement characterizing the capability of the software to perform its required functions under stated conditions for a specified period of time.

restriction—A measurable constraint that sets a limit on compliance during software execution.

robustness—A nonfunctional requirement characterizing the capability of the software to cope with errors during execution.

role—A collection of stakeholders pursuing the same desires while interacting with the software.

scalability—A nonfunctional requirement characterizing the capability of the software to handle growing amounts of work in a graceful manner.

scenario—A short description of an action causing a state transition that confirms an important behavior that is required for the fulfillment of a user story. Formal techniques to script scenarios are the Given-When-Then syntax or the FIT tabular format. Both techniques demonstrate a cause-and-effect behavior from the stakeholders' perspective.

Scrum—An agile software development framework developed by Ken Schwaber and Jeff Sutherland that consists of roles, events, artifacts, and a set of rules that bind them together. Scrum enables development teams to build complex products through frequent inspection and adaptation to optimize output.

security—A nonfunctional requirement characterizing the degree to which the software protects against threats.

self-documenting code—A practice of ensuring code is its own best documentation by allowing useful information, such as programming constructs and logical structure, to be deduced from the naming convention and code layout convention.

simplicity—A nonfunctional requirement characterizing the ease of understanding or explaining.

specification workshop—A meeting that brings together, at the beginning of the sprint, the team and appropriate stakeholders to create a shared understanding of all the scenarios due to be delivered during the sprint.

sprint—A feedback loop lasting less than 30 days during which a product increment is created that enables Scrum teams to inspect and adapt to the stakeholders' changing desirements.

stakeholder—Any person, or group of people, who have an interest in your software who aren't directly involved with its construction. Internal stakeholders have something to gain from the successful completion of the software. These stakeholders are the buyers, the end users, the domain experts, the sales team, the support team, the infrastructure and operations team, the enterprise architecture team, and managers. External stakeholders, such as suppliers, distributers, unions, cities, society, and the government are the ones who can positively or negatively influence the performance of the software upon completion.

state—The conditions of the software before and after the action is performed in a scenario.

storyboard—A rough, even hand-sketched, sequence of drawings that illustrates the important steps of the user experience for the purpose of previsualizing the behavior of a user story.

story mapping—A collaboration board to help plan sprints and order the backlog. It combines high-value and low-value user stories in a coherent set, thereby revealing sprints that are of perceptible value to the stakeholders.

story point—A degree of difficulty numerically summarizing the effort, complexity, and risk.

success criteria—The additional information about the user story that establishes the conditions of acceptance. It enables the team to know when it is done, and it says, in the words of the stakeholders, how it expects to verify the desirable outcome of a user story.

task board—A collaboration board that guides the work of a team during a sprint. It enables team members to see, at a glance, what is done, what remains to be done, and who is working on what.

team—A group of people with complementary skills linked in a common purpose.

test automation framework—A mechanism provided by a general-purpose programming language to hook into and drive the application under test, to execute the tests, and to report results.

test-driven development—A development practice that uses the red/green/refactor cycle for implementing a piece of code with the unit test.

test environment—A clone of the production environment that replicates the minimal functionality needed for executing acceptance tests against the software under construction and for gathering tests results.

test result—A consequence of executing acceptance tests against the software under construction. The result of a test is either pass (green), fail (red) or pending implementation (yellow).

testability—A nonfunctional requirement characterizing the ease of confirming conformance by observing a reproducible behavior.

tester—A developer concerned with automating confirmation with acceptance tests. Testers' main responsibility is to translate scenarios into failing acceptance tests. Testers transpose using an internal DSL the Given-When-Then steps of the scenarios into an acceptance test. They calibrate the failing tests by designing and connecting the programming interface.

trial and error—A heuristic method of problem solving in which only the trials that are most promising tend to be adopted and improved in future trials, whereas those that are less promising tend to be eliminated.

usability—A nonfunctional requirement characterizing the ease with which the software can be used by specified users to achieve specified goals.

user story—A short description of a unit of software that works, delivers value, and generates feedback from stakeholders. The description is written as a one-liner using the classic template: "As a <role>, I want <desire> so that <benefit>." By decoupling roles, desires, and benefits, user stories establish a ubiquitous language that enforces a shared understanding between stakeholders and the development team.

velocity—A number of story points completed during a sprint.

vision—A one-line summary that provides a shared understanding between the team and the stakeholders of what the software is supposed to be and do.

Index

Numbers

80/20 rule, 3

A

Acceptance Test-Driven
    Development (ATDD), 77
acceptance tests, converting
    scenarios to, 98-101
    CI (continuous integration)
        versus, 118-119
    connecting with interface,
        110-114
    enhancing with test results,
        119-120
    implementing the interface,
        115-117
    internal DSL (domain-specific
        language), 104-109
    red-green-refactor cycle,
        101-103
    refactor stage, 117
accessibility
    defined, 125
    testing practice for, 135
actions, defined, 75
adaptation events, 15-16
Adzic, Gojko, 77, 86, 87
agile, origin of term, 1
Agile Estimating and Planning
    (Cohn), 59

agile zone (uncertainty diagram)
    described, 6
    handling uncertainty in, 7-9
analysts
    defined, 149
    product owners versus, 46
    role in specification workshops,
        88-89
anarchy zone (uncertainty
    diagram), described, 6
annotations, 106
architects
    defined, 150
    role in nonfunctional
        requirements, 126
Are Your Lights On? (Weinberg
    and Gauss), 31
assumptions, verifying, 98-101
ATDD (Acceptance Test-Driven
    Development), 77
automating scenario confirmation,
    101-103

B

BDD (Behavior-Driven Develop-
    ment), 77, 79, 105, 107-108
Beck, Kent, 60, 101
benefits in user stories, 38-40
boundaries (guardrails)
    "can-exist" assumption, 22
    common goal, 20
    high-level feature set, 21-22

Executable Specifications with Scrum

A Practical Guide to Agile Requirements Discovery

Mario Cardinal

FREE
Online Edition

Your purchase of **Executable Specifications with Scrum** includes access to a free online edition for 45 days through the Safari Books Online subscription service. Nearly every Addison-Wesley Professional book is available online through Safari Books Online, along with thousands of books and videos from publishers such as Cisco Press, Exam Cram, IBM Press, O'Reilly Media, Prentice Hall, Que, Sams, and VMware Press.

Safari Books Online is a digital library providing searchable, on-demand access to thousands of technology, digital media, and professional development books and videos from leading publishers. With one monthly or yearly subscription price, you get unlimited access to learning tools and information on topics including mobile app and software development, tips and tricks on using your favorite gadgets, networking, project management, graphic design, and much more.

Activate your FREE Online Edition at
informit.com/safarifree

STEP 1: Enter the coupon code: VFDUFWH.

STEP 2: New Safari users, complete the brief registration form.
Safari subscribers, just log in.

If you have difficulty registering on Safari or accessing the online edition,
please e-mail customer-service@safaribooksonline.com

  Addison Wesley AdobePress   ALPHA Cisco Press   FT Press FINANCIAL TIMES IBM Press Microsoft Press New Riders O'REILLY

 Peachpit Press PRENTICE HALL Que Redbooks SAMS SAS Publishing vmware PRESS WILEY wrox